MOLECULES IN THE SERVICE OF MAN

INTRODUCING MODERN SCIENCE

MOLECULES IN THE SERVICE OF MAN A. H. Drummond, Jr.

J.B. LIPPINCOTT COMPANY

Philadelphia and New York

ACKNOWLEDGMENTS

Any book such as this one requires the help of many individuals and institutions. In this particular case, the research goes back some eight to ten years, and includes so many people it will not be possible to list them here. To all, however, I extend sincere thanks. I am also most grateful to my wife Anne and Miss Lorraine Sitewicz for typing the manuscript, and to Mrs. Judith Lavallee for her help with the voluminous correspondence that accompanied development of the manuscript.

A.H.D.

U.S. Library of Congress Cataloging in Publication Data

Drummond, A   H
  Molecules in the service of man.

  SUMMARY: Describes the basic structure of molecules and discusses the problems and progress originating from man's use of special kinds of molecules.
  1. Chemistry—Juvenile literature. [1. Chemistry. 2. Molecules] I. Title.
QD35.D78   540   72-3718
ISBN-0-397-31242-3

This book is for
Laura and Sandy,
whose whimsical
views of their
father as an author
are a constant source
of delight.

CONTENTS

MOLECULES IN THE SERVICE OF MAN

1

ATOMS—The Alphabet Soup of Matter

This book is about molecules—unusual molecules. But to understand any molecules, much less the large and sometimes complex ones we will be talking about, it is necessary to lay some groundwork. We must first explore important basic ideas about atoms, the basic units that make up molecules. We must also become familiar with the forces that hold molecules together, and with some of the different shapes molecules can assume. Then, with these basic ideas safely tucked away, we will be in a position to tackle the curious, unexpected, even bizarre molecules that populate the world of matter.

We will find clawlike molecules that literally grasp their "prey," preventing escape; molecules shaped like cages that trap other particles; molecules that allow some particles to pass through them, but stop others; molecules willing to "make a trade," giving up one kind of particle in exchange for another; and so on. We will also encounter high polymers, those giants of the molecular world that have given us such a remarkable array of goods for the consumer, ranging from rubber through plastics (polyethylene, polystyrene, etc.) to the so-called miracle fabrics (nylon, Dacron, etc.).

The Building Blocks of Matter

The story begins with atoms—the tiny particles that have been called the basic building blocks of matter. The word "atom," meaning indivisible, was invented by the Greeks. The word was first used by Democritus in 460 B.C. when he described the physical world as composed of atoms. We have come a long way since Democritus, but both the word "atom" and the ideas it conveys to chemists have survived. Even today, the chemist's goals may be summed up in very few questions: What atoms are present in a substance? What types of bonds hold the atoms together in a molecule? What shapes do molecules assume, and how does the shape of a molecule affect its chemical behavior? How do atoms and molecules interact with other atoms and molecules? How can we use the products of chemical reactions?

Atoms are very small. They are much too small to be seen by an ordinary microscope. Yet despite their tiny size, the heaviest atom is something more than 200 times as heavy as the lightest atom. Atoms are so small it is difficult to work with their actual weights. Instead, a comparative system of weights is set up, and the weight of any given atom is expressed in terms of a standard. Today the world's scientists all use the carbon-12 standard. In this system, atoms of carbon-12 (atoms with nuclei containing six protons and six neutrons) are arbitrarily assigned the weight value 12. To illustrate, when we speak of the atomic weight of aluminum as 27.0, we mean that N (a symbol representing a given number of atoms) atoms of aluminum are 27.0/12.0 times as heavy as N atoms of carbon-12. It is also true that N hydrogen atoms, each with an atomic weight of about 1.00, are 1.00/27.0 times as heavy as N aluminum atoms and 1.00/12.0 times as heavy as N carbon-12 atoms. In fact, carbon-12 was chosen as the standard for atomic weights partly in order to make the atomic weight of hydrogen, the lightest element, as nearly 1.00 as possible.

Despite the fact that we cannot see or handle atoms individually, many instruments are available to detect them, measure their size, and count them to a very high degree of accuracy. Thus once we know what types of atoms are present in a sample of a substance and how much the substance weighs, we can determine how many atoms there are in the sample. From time to time, as the need arises, we will say more about these instrumental methods.

Literally hundreds of thousands of chemical compounds have been identified and studied. While this number looks impossibly large, it is not, simply because these compounds are made up of just a little over 100 different kinds of atoms—the chemical elements. Only about a third of the elements, however, are found in the substances we come into contact with in everyday life.

The term *element* has a special meaning for the chemist. A substance consisting of only one kind of atom is called an element. Thus a collection of atoms whose nuclei each contain one proton is a sample of the element hydrogen. Similarly, a group of atoms with six protons in each of their nuclei is a sample of the element carbon. Oxygen nuclei contain eight protons each, chlorine nuclei 17 protons, and so on. The number of protons in the nucleus of an atom is the *atomic number* of that atom (element). While it is not particularly important for what we are going to discuss in this book, it is worth noting that the chemical properties of an element depend upon the number of protons in the nuclei of the atoms of that element. It is not surprising that the chemical behavior of hydrogen (one proton) is different from the chemical behavior of oxygen (eight protons).

Chemists, like specialists in many different fields, have had to invent a language to convey chemical information. Chemical language is not very difficult, and it is easily understood once the basic vocabulary—chemical symbols—has been mastered. Chemical symbols represent the elements in both qualitative (what is it?) and quantitative (how much is there?) terms. For our purposes, however, identification of the element will be sufficient.

The symbols for the great majority of the elements are taken from the first letters of the elements' names. Sometimes, to avoid confusion, it is necessary to use the first two letters. The first letter of the symbol is always capitalized, and the second letter is always lower case. Following this convention avoids confusion when the symbols are grouped together to represent chemical compounds (e.g., $NaCl$, SiO_2). Some of the elements have a symbol unrelated to the English name of the element. These symbols were derived, for the most part, from the Latin names of the elements. For example, Fe comes from *ferrum,* Cu from *cuprum,* and Na from *natrium.*

The symbols used in this book are:

Hydrogen	H	Oxygen	O	Sodium	Na
Chlorine	Cl	Carbon	C	Tin	Sn
Nitrogen	N	Nickel	Ni	Magnesium	Mg
Sulfur	S	Argon	Ar	Bromine	Br
Krypton	Kr	Xenon	Xe	Phosphorus	P
Copper	Cu	Iron	Fe	Boron	B
Calcium	Ca	Silicon	Si	Silver	Ag
Aluminum	Al	Potassium	K	Fluorine	F

Compounds

When two or more atoms combine chemically, another type of matter may form—either molecules or crystalline matter. Sometimes, when the atoms combining are alike, as in H_2 and O_2, we have molecules of an element. For the most part, however, the molecules of interest to us will be chemical compounds. In compounds, two or more different atoms have combined to form the molecule—a particle that exists independently of other particles. Some familiar compounds that occur as molecules are ordinary sugar ($C_{12}H_{22}O_{11}$), carbon dioxide (CO_2), and ethyl alcohol (CH_3CH_2OH).

But the molecule is not the only structural form found in nature. Solid structures called *crystals* also exist. To understand how crystals differ from molecules, we must dig a little deeper into the structure of atoms and how they combine chemically.

We now view atoms as consisting of a positively charged nucleus surrounded by a negatively charged field, spherical in shape. In a neutral atom the charge of the positive nucleus just balances the charge of the negative field. The nucleus contains two types of particles, positively charged *protons* and neutral (no charge) *neutrons.* As far as the ordinary chemist is concerned, the nucleus doesn't change. It remains the same throughout all kinds of reactions.

The negatively charged field surrounding the nucleus is made up of electrons. The electrons move about the nucleus at enormously high speeds, held in their paths by electrostatic attraction (the attractive force between unlike charges). The chemist views the electrons as being located in different *energy levels.* Now, while it is possible to detect, locate, and measure individual atoms, it is not possible to do this with individual electrons within an atom. In fact, it is quite impossible to know at the same time the speed and direction of an electron and its location within an atom. What this means very simply is that we cannot talk about electrons *as particles* within an atom. Instead, the chemist talks about the negative field, or charge cloud, that the electron produces as it moves at very high speeds through its energy level space.

When atoms combine, the charge clouds of the electrons in the outermost energy levels are involved. A moment's thought will tell you that this is reasonable. If atoms are spherical, and we think they are, then only the outer electron clouds will be in a position to come into contact when two atoms collide. It should also seem reasonable that atoms can combine only if they collide with sufficient energy to make these outer electron clouds interact.

Electrovalent and Covalent Bonds

In general, two types of electron interaction occur when atoms combine. The first type produces *ionic,* or *electrovalent* bonds, and occurs primarily between metals and nonmetals. Magnesium, iron, and gold are examples of metals, while such substances as oxygen, chlorine, and nitrogen are nonmetals. The overall process can best be described in terms of energy. Metallic atoms have an outer electron cloud made up of only a few electrons, usually fewer than three. But this is an unstable structure in terms of energy. Nonmetallic atoms, on the other hand, have an outer electron cloud very nearly complete. That is, in nonmetallic atoms the outer electron cloud usually lacks only one or two electrons to achieve a particularly stable arrangement. Thus, it is possible to form structures with a greater stability by transferring the outer electrons of metallic atoms to the outer energy levels of nonmetallic atoms. This is exactly what happens.

Consider the reaction between the metal sodium (Na) and the nonmetal chlorine (Cl) to form sodium chloride, ordinary table salt. The sodium atom has a single electron in its outermost energy level, while the chlorine atom's outer energy level lacks but a single electron to give it a particularly stable structure consisting of eight electrons (often called an *octet* of electrons). Now, when a sodium atom collides with a chlorine atom, the conditions are ideal for both atoms to achieve a more stable state. The sodium atom gives up its outer electron, the chlorine atom picks it up, and both atoms are in the more desirable lower energy state.

But this isn't all that happens. When the sodium atom surrenders an electron, it becomes positively charged because the atom now has one more proton than electrons:

$$Na \rightarrow Na^+ + e^-$$

The Na^+ particle is called a sodium *ion,* and the e^- is, of course, an electron. Conversely, when the chlorine atom gains an electron, it becomes negatively charged (a chloride ion) because the atom now has one more electron than protons:

$$Cl + e^- \rightarrow Cl^-$$

But oppositely charged particles attract each other. Hence we find the Na^+ ion and the Cl^- ion attracted to each other and held together by electrostatic attraction. This two-particle structure is an *ion-pair* of sodium chloride [Figure 1-1 (a)]. When four ions come together, we have two ion-pairs of the compound [Figure 1-1 (b)].

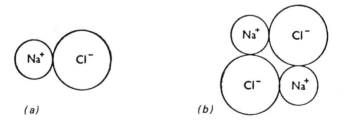

(a)   *(b)*

Figure 1-1.   In ionic bonds electrostatic attraction holds the oppositely charged ions together. The two-particle structure in (*a*) is an ion-pair of sodium chloride. Two ion-pairs are shown in (*b*).

But we never have just one or two pairs of atoms reacting. Thus, when more ion-pairs are formed, they arrange themselves into a so-called *crystal lattice,* with each positive ion surrounded by negative ions and each negative ion surrounded by positive ions. The structure of the sodium chloride crystal lattice is shown in Figure 1-2.

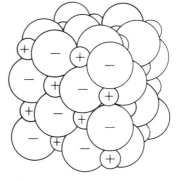

Figure 1-2. Many ion-pairs of sodium chloride as they occur in the crystalline state.

The second major type of electron interaction produces *covalent* bonds. While ionic bonds usually form between atoms of metals and nonmetals, covalent bonds usually occur between atoms of nonmetals. The vast majority of chemical compounds contain covalent bonds. These bonds are also best described in terms of energy.

When two nonmetallic atoms with approximately the same outer-energy-level structure approach each other, there is no energy advantage in the transfer of an electron from one to the other. That is, not enough energy is liberated to make the process occur. In a way, the two atoms are competing for the one or two electrons that will give them a stable outer-energy-level arrangement. Suppose, as in the case of the hydrogen atom, that two electrons in the outer energy level is a particularly stable structure. Atoms of hydrogen (atomic number 1) contain one proton in the nucleus. These atoms therefore have one electron outside the nucleus. But now consider what happens when two hydrogen atoms approach each other with enough force to make the electron clouds interact.

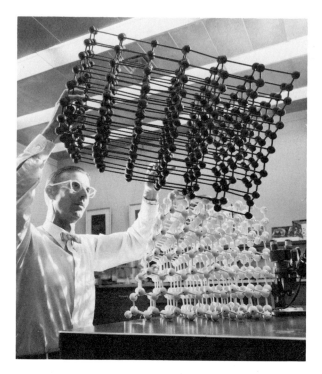

Figure 1-3. Ball and stick models showing the spatial arrangement of carbon atoms in graphite (black) and diamond (white). The bonds between the atoms in these substances are covalent bonds—the atoms of the bond share the bonding electrons equally. (Photo courtesy of GE Research and Development Center)

Hydrogen atom one attracts the electron of hydrogen atom two, but atom two attracts the electron of atom one *with exactly the same force.* The result is an impasse. Neither atom can pull the electron away from the other. Each of the atoms, however, can achieve a more stable arrangement by having two electrons in its outer energy level. The impasse is resolved by *sharing* the two electrons between the two atoms. As this shared-electron-pair bond forms, energy is released. Thus, the molecule is more stable than the individual atoms. Using dots to represent the bonding electrons, the formation of this covalent bond is shown as follows:

$$H\cdot + \cdot H \longrightarrow H:H$$

The chemist pictures the hydrogen molecule in the following terms. The two nuclei approach each other just closely enough for the electron cloud of the combined electrons to surround them. This is a more stable arrangement than that of the separated atoms with a single electron each.

The hydrogen atom, however, is the only one to form covalent bonds with two electrons in the outer energy level. Most atoms form covalent bonds with eight electrons (the octet, again) in the outer energy level. Consider the chlorine molecule. The outer energy level of a chlorine atom contains seven electrons. Clearly, if two chlorine atoms combine, greater stability can be attained if the two atoms share one pair of electrons.

$$:\ddot{C}l\cdot + \cdot\ddot{C}l: \longrightarrow :\ddot{C}l : \ddot{C}l:$$

In this condition, each atom has full possession of six electrons, and shares a pair equally with the other atom. The result is a stable octet for each atom.

Sometimes double bonds, in which two pairs of electrons are shared, form between atoms. Again, greater stability is achieved by the formation of an octet of electrons for each atom. The oxygen molecule, O_2, is often written to contain a double bond, although there is evidence that the molecule contains unpaired electrons. Oxygen atoms have six electrons in the outer energy level. The double bond is shown as follows:

$$\dot{O}\cdot + :\ddot{O}: \longrightarrow \ddot{O}: :\ddot{O}$$

Triple bonds are also known. In addition, we should note that the eight-electron outer energy level is not the only stable arrangement. While fewer in number, ten, twelve, and fourteen-electron outer energy levels are known.

Water—H₂O or Something Else?

Now let's consider the water molecule. Everyone knows that water is H_2O. This is what you learned in school, this is what you read, and this is what you hear. But, as the old song goes, "it ain't necessarily so." Chemists, long intrigued by the puzzling properties of water, have just recently found that it isn't really H_2O at all. Oh, when you get right down to it, all samples of liquid water contain two hydrogen atoms for each oxygen atom. But what the chemists have just found out is that there are very few, if any, individual H_2O molecules in liquid water. But let's start at the beginning, and work up to this recent finding. Curiously enough, even today scientists are discovering things they could just as easily have found ten, twenty, or more years ago if they had been in the right frame of mind.

We really must label H_2O a strange molecule, for while it probably does not exist in liquid water, it seems to be the only particle present in water vapor. It consists of two hydrogen atoms and one oxygen atom, held together by covalent bonds. The molecule has about the same shape as a boomerang (although the similarity ends right there), with the H atoms at the ends and the O atom at the center. Since oxygen atoms have six outer electrons and hydrogen atoms have only a single outer electron, two electron-pair bonds give the oxygen atom an octet of electrons and give each hydrogen atom a pair of electrons.

$$\overset{\displaystyle H}{:\!\ddot{\underset{..}{O}}\!: H}$$

As mentioned, the molecule is shaped more like a boomerang than like the right angle shown above. In fact, the angle between the hydrogen atoms is about 105°, rather than 90°.

This expanded angle is easily accounted for. Think of the oxygen nucleus with its eight protons and the hydrogen nuclei with a single proton each. The oxygen nucleus obviously exerts a greater attractive force on the bonding electrons than the hydrogen nuclei. As a result these electrons are pulled over closer to the oxygen nucleus, leaving the hydrogen nuclei somewhat "naked," or devoid of electrons. But it is only the electrons that shift. The hydrogen nuclei, being much more massive, and also being repelled by the positive oxygen nucleus, resist moving closer to the oxygen nucleus with the electrons. This, of course, exposes the positive hydrogen nuclei to each other, and they move apart by mutual repulsion to the 105° angle.

But this isn't all. The water molecule, like a great many others, has its internal positive and negative charges unequally balanced. Expressed another way, the center of positive charge from the protons does not coincide with the center of negative charge from the electron cloud. Such molecules are said to be *polar.* They have a positive end and a negative end. The total charge on the molecule is zero, however, for there are an equal number of protons and electrons.

The oxygen end of the water molecule is negative, and the hydrogen end is positive, as you have probably figured out by now.

This polarity is why water is not H_2O in the liquid state. When water molecules approach each other, the positive hydrogen arms are attracted to the negative oxygen sites of nearby molecules. As a result, the molecules line up as shown in Figure 1-4. The dashed lines between hydrogen atoms and adjacent oxygen atoms are the result of this attraction. They are called *hydrogen bonds.* Hydrogen bonds are relatively weak bonds held together by electrostatic attraction. They are also three-dimensional, holding the individual water molecules together in a large clump.

Chemists have known for a long time that these clumps of H_2O molecules are present in liquid water. What wasn't known was just how much of a given sample of liquid water is in the clump form, and how much is in the form of individual molecules. Some authorities held that as much as 30 percent is in the monomer (individual molecule) form. Others felt that this figure is too high, and that most of the molecules in a given volume are in the polymeric (clumped) form.

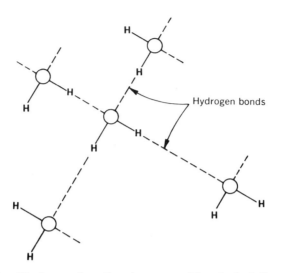

Figure 1-4.   Hydrogen bonding in water. The dashed lines represent weak electrostatic bonds between a hydrogen atom and a nearby oxygen atom.

Recent work has solved the problem. The question should have been laid to rest many years ago, however, for the necessary tools have been available right along. The problem was attacked in three different ways. First, the absorption of ultraviolet light by both liquid water and water vapor was measured. The absorption pattern of the vapor (all individual molecules) should also appear in the liquid to the extent that individual molecules exist in the liquid. The results showed that only about 0.1 percent free water molecules are present in liquid water.

Next, the absorption of infrared radiation by liquid water and dilute solutions of water in chloroform and carbon tetrachloride were compared. The water molecules do not form hydrogen bonds in chloroform and carbon tetrachloride solutions, thus they are free and can be used as a basis for comparison. The absorption patterns were quite different, showing that liquid water contains no free molecules within the limits of error of the experiment, about one percent.

Finally, certain properties of the vaporization of water were compared with the same properties of substances such as natural gas (methane, CH_4) and the rare gases (e.g., argon, xenon), which are known to have free molecules in the liquid state. The calculations here indicated only about 0.2 percent free H_2O molecules in liquid water.

Thus liquid water isn't H_2O after all. It is really $H_{2n}O_n$, with n unknown. Very likely many clumps of $H_{2n}O_n$ exist within a given sample of liquid water. The next time you slake your thirst with a long drink of iced water, remember that it isn't billions of individual water molecules you are swallowing, but rather many giant clumps of H_2O molecules held together by hydrogen bonds.

2
CLATHRATES—Caged Molecules

Water vapor is a gas containing free H_2O molecules, liquid water is fluid and flexible—the molecules are loosely bound together in large clumps —and ice, a solid, contains the same H_2O molecules, but this time in a rigid three-dimensional structure. In ice each H_2O molecule has four immediate neighbors, with each oxygen atom surrounded by four other oxygen atoms at the corners of a tetrahedron. The whole thing is held together by hydrogen bonds—once again represented by dashed lines in Figure 2-1.

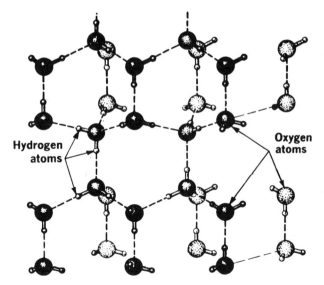

Figure 2-1. The three-dimensional structure of ice. The water molecules are held in place by hydrogen bonds.

But notice, if we move the molecules closer to each other, distinct small volumes surrounded by groups of molecules appear. It doesn't take too much imagination to picture these groups of molecules as cages, although they are probably the oddest looking cages you have ever seen.

The cagelike property of the molecules in ice is not particularly important. There are no applications or far-reaching implications to speak of. Other molecules, however, including some that contain water, form unique cages. They are called clathrates, from the Latin word *clathratus,* meaning enclosed or protected by cross bars or grating.

Molecular cages were first suspected as far back as 1811, when the English scientist Humphrey Davy made an interesting discovery. He had been investigating a compound thought to be crystalline chlorine. To his surprise, he found that the substance contained water.

Twelve years later Faraday was able to report further on the compound's composition. He found it to be chlorine hydrate, a crystalline substance containing chlorine molecules trapped in a complex network of water molecules. Faraday's calculations indicated that the simplest formula for chlorine hydrate was $Cl_2 \cdot 10H_2O$. That is, for each chlorine molecule there are ten water molecules in the crystal. Today we honor the insight of these early workers—at that time chemistry didn't even have a fully workable theory of atoms and chemical combination —but we also recognize their limitations. By means of detailed x-ray study, we now know the composition of chlorine hydrate is closer to $Cl_2 \cdot 8H_2O$. It has an interesting structure.

Forty-six water molecules make up the smallest repeating unit in the crystal, the so-called unit cell. The water molecules, held together by hydrogen bonds, form the corners of two types of cages (polyhedra) inside the unit cell. Twenty molecules form the corners of a pentagonal dodecahedron (Figure 2-2).

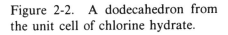

Figure 2-2. A dodecahedron from the unit cell of chlorine hydrate.

As you can see, this polyhedron has 12 pentagonal (five-sided) faces. There are two such dodecahedra per unit cell. These forty water molecules, plus six more, are held together by hydrogen bonds such that they outline six tetrakaidecahedra in addition to the two dodecahedra per unit cube. Tetrakaidecahedra are polyhedra with two hexagonal (six-sided) faces and twelve pentagonal faces.

A portion of the chlorine hydrate crystal is shown in Figure 2-3.

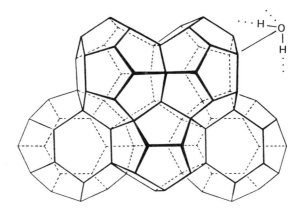

Figure 2-3. A portion of the chlorine hydrate crystal. As shown, water molecules occupy the corners of the polyhedra.

This sketch shows how the dodecahedra fit in with the tetrakaidecahedra. The orientation of a water molecule at the corner of one of the polyhedra, along with the hydrogen bonds it forms, is also shown.

Now for the occupants of these terribly confusing cages. Chlorine molecules occupy the tetrakaidecahedra, being too large for the dodecahedra. Thus, there are six Cl_2 molecules per unit cell of the hydrate. In addition, experimental evidence indicates that two more H_2O molecules are located in each unit cell. They reside in the two dodecahedra. Adding it all up, we get 46 plus the two extra water molecules, a total of 48, and six chlorine molecules. The ratio for the crystal as a whole is therefore eight water molecules to one chlorine molecule, or $Cl_2 \cdot 8H_2O$. Someone many years ago suggested that the trapped molecules be called "guest" particles, and the crystal cages the "host." The names stuck, and we now find ourselves describing a kind of chemical "party" when we talk about clathrates.

Trapped But Not Chemically Bound

The particles trapped in a molecular cage are not chemically bonded to the atoms forming the cage. They are simply trapped there because they are too large to slip out through the openings in the cage. They would slip out if the holes were large enough.

All matter is in a constant state of motion. The particles in clathrates are no exception. In solids the particles vibrate over short distances within a fixed region in space. In liquids the distances and volumes are greater. In gases they are greater yet. Thus, in clathrates both the guest and host particles are in constant vibratory motion. Unless something unusual happens, however, the guest particles must remain trapped within the host crystal.

The structural details of the chlorine hydrate crystal make it clear that clathrates are anything but simple. The chemist working with these substances thus has a difficult task—he must first understand the highly complex structure he is working with, and then he must somehow communicate what he has learned to others.

A wide variety of clathrates is possible. For example, when the organic compound hydroquinone, $C_6H_4(OH)_2$, which has the structure shown in Figure 2-4, is allowed to crystallize from an evaporating aqueous solution in the presence of the gas argon, an interesting clathrate forms. The resulting crystalline solid has all the properties of hydroquinone, but it contains trapped argon. To release the argon one merely has to melt or dissolve the solid hydroquinone.

The unit cell, or cage, of the hydroquinone clathrate contains three hydroquinone molecules for each guest particle, its general formula being $[C_6H_4(OH)_2]_3X$. The X, of course, represents the trapped guest particle. It will come as no surprise to find out that this cage lattice is also held together by hydrogen bonds.

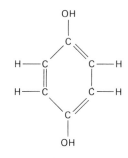

Figure 2-4.   The structure of the
hydroquinone molecule.

Argon isn't the only gas to form clathrates with hydroquinone. Others include the familiar sulfur dioxide (SO_2), hydrogen chloride (HC1), hydrogen sulfide (H_2S), and carbon dioxide (CO_2).

An even more interesting clathrate can be made from nickel cyanide, ammonia, and benzene. If benzene (C_6H_6) is added to a solution of nickel cyanide [Ni $(CN)_2$] in ammonia (NH_3) and agitated vigorously, a pale mauve colored clathrate forms. This time, however, instead of the organic compound (benzene) forming the cage, it is the inorganic system that becomes the cage. As the diagram shows, the nickel cyanide and ammonia molecules form the lattice, with benzene molecules trapped inside (Figure 2-5).

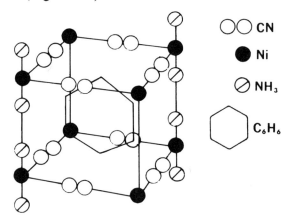

Figure 2-5.   How the benzene molecule becomes trapped in a lattice consisting of ammonia and nickel cyanide molecules.

By now, you must be wondering how these unusual substances can exist. As it turns out, very special conditions must be met for them to form.

Conditions for Clathrate Formation

First, the host crystal must have an open structure in the solid state. For this to happen, the bonds between the atoms in the crystal must point in specific directions. There must also be a minimum bond length. Any bond shorter than this minimum would not permit the enclosed volume to form. Clearly, the molecular framework must also be rigid. Without rigidity, the lattice would collapse, eliminating the cage spaces.

Second, the access holes to the cavities within the crystal must be small. If they are too large, guest particles cannot be trapped. They simply pass through, just as grains of sand go through an ordinary sieve. This explains why some substances form clathrates, while others do not.

Third, the guest particle must be present when the cage cavity closes. Sometimes this is brought about easily. Often, however, special physical conditions must be imposed to get the host and guest together. For example, in the argon-hydroquinone clathrate mentioned earlier, the argon must be present at a pressure of 40 atmospheres (forty times sea-level pressure) for the clathrate to form.

Finally, it is volume available and not the chemical nature of the particles involved that determines the type of guest particle to be enclosed. For example, we saw earlier that Cl_2 molecules occupy the tetrakaidecahedra of the chlorine hydrate crystal, being too large to fit inside the dodecahedra. H_2O molecules, however, do fit inside the dodecahedra. Sometimes experimental data yields unexpected dividends. In this case, we see immediately that Cl_2 molecules are somewhat larger than H_2O molecules, confirming evidence obtained from quite different experiments.

"Packaging" at the Molecular Level

Zeolites, an interesting class of aluminosilicates that we will say more about in Chapter Three, now seem to offer the clathrate chemist a unique new application. Before describing this new possibility, which for want of a better term we will call "molecular packaging," it is necessary to outline zeolite structure.

The basic structural group in zeolites is a tetrahedron consisting of silicon and oxygen atoms. See Figure 2-6.

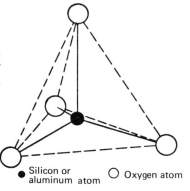

Figure 2-6. The basic structural group of zeolites—the silicon (or aluminum) and oxygen tetrahedron.

● Silicon or aluminum atom   ○ Oxygen atom

This basic group is incorporated into a three-dimensional polymer joined together by oxygen bonds. In zeolites some of the silicon atoms have been replaced by aluminum atoms. Thus, in Figure 2-7, the dark circles may be either silicon or aluminum atoms. If you look closely, you can distinguish the tetrahedral shape of each structural group.

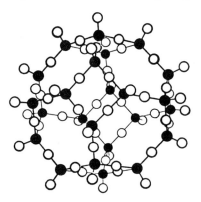

Figure 2-7. How the silicon-oxygen tetrahedra combine to form the three-dimensional zeolite structure.

Once again, however, it is desirable to simplify. The confusion of Figure 2-7 can be eliminated almost completely, revealing the cagelike structure of the crystal, by substituting geometric tetrahedra for the "ball and stick" tetrahedra. See Figure 2-8.

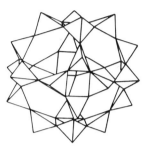

Figure 2-8. The result of substituting geometric tetrahedra for "ball and stick" tetrahedra.

This concept is clearly quite a bit easier to work with.

The shape and size of the openings in zeolite crystals relative to the total internal volume available is the key to molecular packaging. Look at the diagrams of the two zeolites shown in Figure 2-9. Note how the internal volume of each cage is larger than any of the openings to the outside.

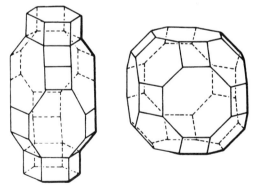

Figure 2-9. The simplest way to represent zeolite structure. Straight lines join the locations of the atoms that outline the shape of the crystal. Note the different sizes and shapes of the openings in the cages.

Now suppose we have a particle small enough to fit inside these cages, but too large to pass through any of the openings. All we would have to do is get the guest particle inside—once there, it would stay. It now looks as if this can be done. Heating the zeolite crystal would cause the lattice atoms to vibrate more vigorously over greater distances, thus opening up the pores. If the desired guest particles are present, especially under high pressure, they should enter the crystal. Then, when the lattice is allowed to cool, they would be trapped—"packaged," so to speak.

We can imagine all kinds of applications for this technique. For example, suppose you want to store a highly explosive gas in your laboratory, but you are afraid of the danger. If the gas could be supplied in clathrate form, the individual gas molecules would be separated from one another within an inert medium. This should vastly reduce the danger of explosion.

How about the possibility of transporting dangerous chemicals as clathrates? Could the highly flammable hydrogen fuel used in the fuel cells of manned spacecraft be stored in clathrate form until needed?

Chemical engineers might also get some use out of clathrates. For example, it is often desirable to control the rate of a key reaction in a chemical synthesis. If one of the reactants was supplied in clathrate form, it could be carried to the reaction chamber and released at precisely the rate desired by the chemical engineer.

3

ZEOLITES – Molecular Sieves

Almost everyone knows that spaghetti is cooked by boiling it in water. But then, to separate the spaghetti from the water before serving it, the cook pours everything into a sieve called a colander. The water pours through the holes in the colander, but the spaghetti is trapped.

What does spaghetti have to do with molecular sieves? Well, in a very general way we can look on the spaghetti and water mixture as a mixture of two types of molecules with different sizes and shapes; the colander in turn may be compared to a molecular sieve. When the mixture of molecules (spaghetti and water) is brought into contact with the molecular sieve (the colander), the mixture is effectively separated.

There are serious inaccuracies, however, with this analogy. One of the largest is the fact that the holes in the colander are in a sheet of metal, while in a molecular sieve the holes are pores and cavities within a three-dimensional crystal. We can improve the analogy by suggesting a rather far-out way to drain the spaghetti. Instead of using a colander, pour the spaghetti and boiling water onto a large sponge. The result? Now the sponge absorbs the water but refuses to take up the strands of spaghetti. This, on a large scale, is pretty much what seems to happen in a molecular sieve (Figure 3-1).

The utility of molecular sieves, of course, comes from the fact that they can be used to separate mixtures of molecules of different sizes and shapes. As a result, they have become the object of major commercial interest in recent years. For example, the petroleum industry has found molecular sieves to be useful in their attempts to increase the octane rating of gasoline. Certain molecular sieves absorb very large amounts of straight-chain hydrocarbon molecules, while rejecting branched-chain hydrocarbons. As you may know, the greater the quantity of

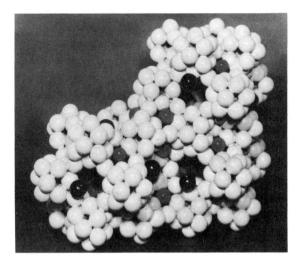

Figure 3-1. Model of the molecular structure of a typical zeolite. Note the openings leading to the outside, and how the structure produces a network of cavities within the solid. (Photo courtesy of D. W. Breck, Union Carbide Corp.; reprinted with permission from *J. Chem. Educ.,* **41,** 678 (1964))

branched-chain hydrocarbons in a gasoline, the higher its octane rating. In another example, the detergent industry has found use for molecular sieves in the development of biodegradable detergents.

From "Boiling Stone" to Zeolite

These and other interesting new applications of molecular sieves stem from newly acquired knowledge about *zeolites,* the crystalline compounds mentioned in the last chapter in connection with "molecular packaging." The zeolites, all aluminosilicates, are characterized by a very open structure, with a network of channels running throughout. Natural zeolites are sometimes called *boiling stones* (from the Greek *zeo,* meaning to boil, and *lithos,* meaning stone). The term *boiling stones,* which was first used several centuries ago, suggests one of the curious properties of zeolites. If they are heated strongly, they sometimes seem to boil and melt at the same time. This occurs because water is being driven rapidly out of the crystalline structure.

If the same zeolites are heated gently, however, the water is driven off without altering the basic crystalline framework. This framework is rigid and porous on the molecular level. When allowed to cool in this anhydrous condition, the porous crystal will either reabsorb water, or other vapors that might be present in place of water. Thus, with water driven off, the zeolites have greater absorbing capacity. In addition, the occurrence of different sized pores and channels within the crystal offers a unique selectivity. As mentioned, it is possible to actually select a zeolite that will absorb one kind of molecule but reject others.

Zeolite structure offers one possible explanation to these unique properties. As mentioned in the previous chapter, the basic building block of any zeolite crystal is a tetrahedron of oxygen ions (O^{2-}) surrounding a smaller silicon (Si^{4+}) or aluminum (Al^{3+}) ion. See Figure 3-2.

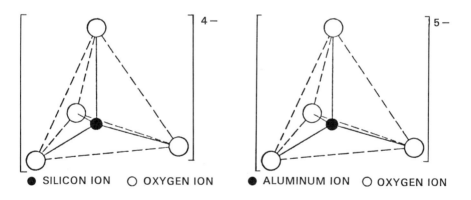

● SILICON ION   ○ OXYGEN ION   ● ALUMINUM ION   ○ OXYGEN ION

Figure 3-2.   The basic building blocks of zeolites. In a zeolite crystal the oxygen ions of each tetrahedron are shared with four other tetrahedra.

As shown, the oxygen ions carry two negative charges, the silicon ion four positive charges, and the aluminum ion three positive charges.

Thus, in the silicon tetrahedron, the charge on each silicon ion offsets half the eight negative charges of the four oxygen ions; the total charge on the tetrahedral unit is minus four. In the aluminum tetrahedron, the charge on the aluminum ion satisfies only three of the eight oxygen negative charges; the net charge on the tetrahedral unit is minus five.

The zeolite crystal is built up by each tetrahedron sharing its oxygen ions with four other tetrahedra. Put another way, each oxygen ion with its negative charge combines with a silicon or aluminum ion from another tetrahedron. The crystal lattice thus extends in all directions. A special case occurs when an aluminum ion is at the center of a zeolite tetrahedron. Because the aluminum ion carries a charge of plus three, an extra positive charge is needed to produce a stable crystalline structure. This extra positive charge occurs in the form of *exchangeable ions;* these cations (positively charged ions) attach themselves loosely to the oxygen ions at the corners of the tetrahedra.

The openings leading to the interior of zeolite crystals are formed by rings of linked tetrahedra. Thus, they are actually rings of oxygen ions. Figure 3-3 illustrates a model of a zeolite surface. Each opening in the surface consists of an 8-membered ring of oxygen ions.

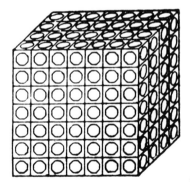

Figure 3-3. Model of a zeolite surface. Each opening in the surface is an eight-membered oxygen ring.

The oxygen ions in turn reside at the corners of tetrahedra. Thus, if the positions of the oxygens surrounding the pores are known, we also know the positions in space of the tetrahedra to which the oxygen ions belong. The number of oxygen ions making up the external openings of a zeolite crystal may vary from four to twelve. The 4- and 5-membered rings are much too small for use as molecular sieves, but the 6-, 8-, 10-, and 12-membered rings offer a wide range of useful applications.

The framework of silicon-oxygen and aluminum-oxygen tetrahedra in zeolite crystals forms a structure that is honeycombed with relatively large cavities. The shape and size of these cavities and the size and number of openings leading into them depend upon the type of zeolite. For example, Figure 3-4 shows two typical zeolite cavities drawn to the same scale. Note that in both cases the external opening is smaller than the internal cavity. In (a) the smaller octahedral windows make the crystal useful as a molecular sieve. In (b), however, the larger 12-sided openings permit the entry of metal-containing compounds. Thus, catalyst metals can be substituted in the tetrahedra for exchangeable ions. This property permits the crystal to serve as a catalyst carrier.

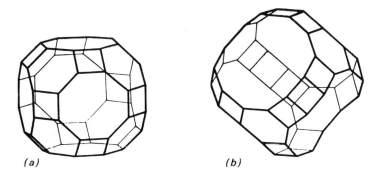

(a)   (b)

Figure 3-4. Typical zeolite cavities drawn to the same scale. Different potential uses depend upon the size of the internal cavity.

In operation, molecular sieves seem to do just what the name implies. On the molecular level, the sieve consists of pores and channels within the aluminosilicate crystalline framework. Knowledge of this structure leads us to the two factors that apparently contribute to a zeolite crystal's selectivity as a molecular sieve. First, there is the size of the external pores. In any given application, all molecules too large to pass through an external pore will be excluded from the interior network of channels. Molecular shape is also important. An example already mentioned is the crystal that readily absorbs straight-chain hydrocarbons, but rejects cyclic or branched-chain hydrocarbon molecules.

Sponge Analogy Inadequate

The amount of space available within a zeolite crystal can be estimated by the volume of water driven out by heating. Sometimes the internal volume amounts to 50 percent or more of the total volume of the crystal, suggesting the main reason why chemists are so interested in these substances. For example, consider a crystal with 46 percent of the total volume available. If we were to spread out in a monolayer the molecules one gram of this crystal can hold, the monolayer would cover some 750 to 800 square meters of area. As good as our sponge analogy may be, it doesn't even approach the total absorptive capacity of a real zeolite crystal!

An alternate theory of the action of molecular sieves rejects the sponge analogy completely! Proponents of the new theory suggest that separations using molecular sieves take place on the crystalline surface, and are caused by strong electrostatic forces, rather than by the passage of smaller molecules into the interior of the zeolite crystal. According to this theory, molecular sieves possess strong electric fields that interact with and attract certain molecules to the surface of the crystal more strongly than others. This attraction accounts for the capability of the zeolite to separate mixtures of molecules. For example, oxygen and nitrogen molecules are comparable in size and small enough to fit into the channels of a zeolite crystal. They are separated by a molecular sieve, however—a fact that cannot be explained by the pore- and channel-size theory. Other evidence for the surface-force theory is the fact that polar, unsaturated, and aromatic molecules may be separated by molecular sieves. These separations seem to be the result of strong, localized positive charges on the crystalline surface that attract the negative ends of polar or polarizable molecules.

We can gain an understanding of these surface forces by looking closely at the structure of a typical zeolite. In the diagram of a portion of the zeolite analcite shown in Figure 3-5, the tetrahedra are shown in relation to water molecules (the larger spheres) and sodium ions (the smaller spheres).

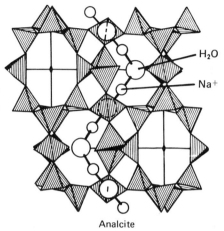

Figure 3-5. Structure of the zeolite analcite. The surface-force theory has its basis in the sodium ions that occupy the channels. See the text for details.

H_2O

Na^+

Analcite

Remember that the sodium ions are present because the charge on aluminum ions (Al^{3+}) offsets one less than half of the total negative charges from the four oxygen ions (O^{2-}) in an aluminum-containing tetrahedron. Now, when the water molecules have been driven out by heating, only the sodium ions occupy the channels of the crystal. But being alone in the channels, with no compensating charge, the sodium ions produce a strong electrostatic field. This is probably the source of the forces described in the surface-force theory.

From Theory to Practical Applications

Numerous useful applications for molecular sieves are emerging as chemists learn more about these interesting substances. For example, in zeolites containing aluminum tetrahedra, the structure carries as many negative charges as there are aluminum ions. These charges are then neutralized by the inclusion of positive ions in the channels within the crystal. But these positive ions can be replaced by other cations. As a result, zeolites are important ion-exchangers (see Chapter Five).

This ion-exchange capability seems to explain the behavior of the zeolite sodium chabazite. In this crystal, sodium ions block the 8-membered openings so that only very small molecules can enter. If these sodium ions are replaced by calcium ions (half as many, because of the two-to-one charge ratio), the openings are no longer blocked and larger molecules may enter, improving the crystal's potential as a molecular sieve.

Another interesting development is the use of zeolites as a water softener. As you may know, the principal ions present in "hard" water are calcium (Ca^{2+}), magnesium (Mg^{2+}), and iron (Fe^{2+} and Fe^{3+}). These ions react with soap to form an insoluble scum. As a result, "soft" water is preferred by housewives. Now, in a typical aluminosilicate, numerous sodium ions are loosely bound up within the crystalline network. When hard water is allowed to flow over zeolite grains, some of the sodium ions of the zeolite are replaced by calcium, magnesium, and iron ions. The net effect is substitution of sodium ions for the hard water ions, and a "softening" of the water. The zeolite crystal, of course, is not soluble. Hence it does not affect the water in any way. After the sodium ions have been exhausted from the crystal, the zeolite is regenerated by soaking it in a saturated brine solution. In this soak the reaction is reversed, and sodium ions replace the hard water ions within the crystalline network.

One of the most important uses of zeolite molecular sieves is the removal of water from gas streams—mixtures of gases flowing through pipes. First the zeolite's own water is driven out. The anhydrous crystal is then used to remove water vapor from a gas it is contaminating. Zeolites have also been found to act as catalysts; in some instances, they have even been used as a carrier for volatile catalysts.

4

CHELATES–Molecular Pincers

If you've ever had a toe nipped by a crab while swimming, you have a pretty good idea of how chelates work. These unusual molecules do almost the same thing as the crab, but at the molecular level. They form rings—chelate rings—that grasp and hold metallic ions very tightly. Remarkable as it may seem, the ions are held so tightly they cannot even be detected after having been seized by the chelating agent.

The term chelate comes from the Greek word *chele,* meaning claw. Thus the crab claw analogy is a good one. Very likely it occurred immediately to the first chemists to work out the nature of these molecules. When a chelating agent is introduced into a solution containing a dissolved metal, it is said to sequester (render inactive) the metal. Clearly, if the metallic ions have been rendered inactive, they cannot be detected if such detection depends upon their reacting with some other chemical reagent. For all practical purposes, the chemical influence of the metallic ions has been eliminated.

The use of chelates has grown very rapidly in recent years. Many new and interesting applications have been developed. For example, chelates are now used in chemical analysis, water softening, agriculture, metal cleaning, and so on. In every instance, a clawlike molecular ring seizes the undesirable metallic ion, making it chemically inactive.

Coordinate Bonds the Key

The bonds between the active atoms in the chelate ring and a metallic ion are covalent bonds. They are, however, a unique type of covalent bond. As you recall, a covalent bond consists of a shared pair of electrons between two atoms. Ordinarily, one of the electrons in the pair comes from each of the atoms. But there is no physical law restricting covalent bonds to this type. Sometimes a covalent bond is formed by one of the atoms supplying both of the electrons of the shared pair. It's still a covalent bond, although its properties differ slightly from the first type we discussed. Bonds in which one atom supplies both of the electrons of the shared pair are called *coordinate bonds.* It's important to note that even though a coordinate bond is formed by a different mechanism, once it has been formed it is not much different from any other covalent bond.

Thus to find coordinate bonds, we must look for atoms in molecules that contain unshared pairs of electrons in the bonding energy levels. Ammonia, NH_3, is a molecule containing such an atom. When ammonia is bubbled through water, a hydrogen ion (proton) is transferred from a water molecule to an ammonia molecule:

$$H\!:\!\ddot{N}\!:\!H + H\!:\!\ddot{O}\!: \longrightarrow H\!:\!\ddot{N}\!:\!H \overset{H^{+}}{} + \ :\!\ddot{O}\!:\!H^{-}$$

We might say the naked electron pair of the nitrogen atom in the ammonia molecule exerts a greater attractive force on the proton than the electron pair of the water molecule. Or we can put it in terms of energy. The NH_4^+ and OH^- arrangement is more stable (has a lower energy content) than the NH_3 and H_2O arrangement.

For another example of the nature of coordinate bonding, consider *hydrates.* Metallic ions in water solutions are said to be hydrated. Figure 4-1 shows how the positively charged metallic ion is surrounded by water molecules, with the negative ends of the water molecules pointing in toward the ion. As you recall, water molecules are bent at an angle of about 105°, with the oxygen atom located at the bend. Thus, when positive ions are hydrated, the oxygen ends of the water molecules with their unshared pairs of electrons point toward the ions.

Two types of bonding forces seem to play a role in hydrates. First, there is electrostatic attraction between the positive ion and the negative end of the water molecule. This is called ion-dipole attraction,

Figure 4-1. How the negative
ends of dipolar water molecules
surround a positive ion in solution.

water being a dipole. Second, there is good evidence that coordinate
bonding is also present. The water molecule donates, and shares, a pair
of its unshared electrons with the ion. Just as in the ammonia plus water
example, the hydrated ions are more stable than the separated ions and
water molecules.

But now suppose a substance that reacts more readily than water
with the ion is added to the system. As expected, the water molecules
will be replaced, producing a different complex ion. For example, consider the familiar blue solution of copper sulfate, $CuSO_4$. This blue
color is a characteristic of solutions of the doubly charged copper ion,
Cu^{2+}. Now, if we add some ammonia to the Cu^{2+} solution, the color
immediately changes to a much deeper blue, indicating that chemical
reaction has taken place. See Figure 4-2. The ammonia molecules in-

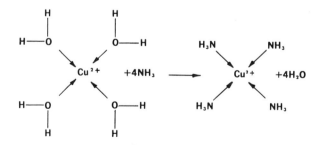

Figure 4-2. The result of adding ammonia (NH_3) to a solution of
Cu^{2+} ion. A change in color reveals that NH_3 groups have replaced the
water molecules originally surrounding the copper ion.

teract more strongly with the copper ions than the water molecules did, hence they replace the water molecules, forming a new complex. Instead of hydrated copper ions, we now have ammoniated copper ions. In this diagram the arrows show the atoms from which the electron pairs come.

Conditions for Chelation

Now let's consider chelation, which is nothing more than a special case of this type of reaction. Three conditions must be met if a molecule is to act as a chelating agent. First, it must contain atoms with available unshared pairs of electrons—oxygen, nitrogen, or sulfur atoms, usually. Second, there must be at least two of these electron-pair donors in the molecule. Finally, there must be a molecular chain long enough for the electron-pair donor atoms to fold in on the metallic ion, forming a ring when bonding takes place.

One simple chelating agent is ethylenediamine. This imposing name is really a lot simpler than it looks. The molecule consists of two (di = two) amine groups ($-NH_2$) connected by an ethylene bridge ($-CH_2CH_2-$). Its formula is thus $H_2NCH_2CH_2NH_2$. If we add ethylenediamine to a solution of Cu^{2+} ions, two ethylenediamine molecules sequester the copper ion, forming a double ring structure (Figure 4-3).

Figure 4-3. The double ring structure produced when a Cu^{2+} ion is sequestered by ethylene diamine.

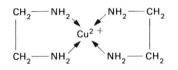

As the diagram suggests, one of the most important factors in chelation is the nature of the ring formed. The molecular chain of the arms of the ring must be long enough for folding without mechanical interference. It must also be long enough so that excessive strain (bending) on the bonds does not prevent the electron-pair donor atoms from interacting with the metallic ions.

Chelating agents such as ethylenediamine, with two electron-pair donor atoms, are said to be *bidentate* (as you see, the biting claw analogy extends even to description of the type of chelation that occurs). When there are three and four donor atoms, respectively, the molecules are referred to as *tridentate* and *tetradentate*. To illustrate, in Figure 4-4 the electron-pair donor atoms are starred.

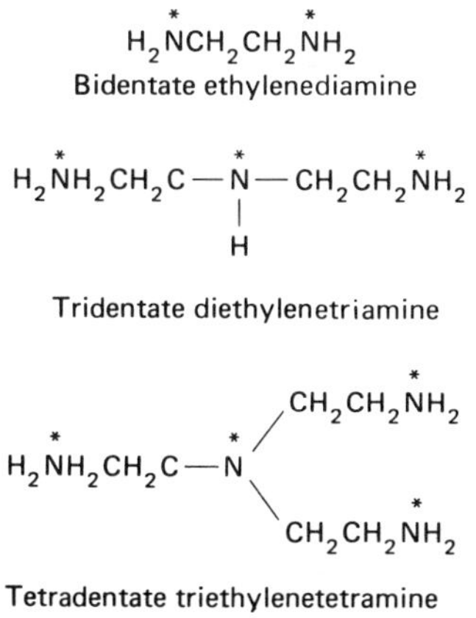

$$H_2 \overset{*}{N}CH_2CH_2\overset{*}{N}H_2$$

Bidentate ethylenediamine

Figure 4-4. The stars indicate the electron-pair donor atoms in typical bidentate, tridentate, and tetradentate chelating agents.

$$H_2\overset{*}{N}H_2CH_2C-\overset{*}{N}-CH_2CH_2\overset{*}{N}H_2$$
$$|$$
$$H$$

Tridentate diethylenetriamine

$$H_2\overset{*}{N}H_2CH_2C-\overset{*}{N}\overset{\diagup CH_2CH_2\overset{*}{N}H_2}{\diagdown CH_2CH_2\overset{*}{N}H_2}$$

Tetradentate triethylenetetramine

As you may have suspected, there is an increase in metal-donor bond strength as the number of electron-pair donor atoms in the chelating molecule increases. Thus, the bond formed by ethylenediamine (one ring) is less stable than the bond formed by diethylenetriamine (two rings). This in turn is less stable than the bond formed by triethylenetetramine (three rings). This increase in chemical stability as the number of bonding atoms in the chelating molecules increases is called the *chelate effect*. It is a simple means of classifying the relative chelating strength of different substances.

One of the most powerful and useful chelating agents known goes by the tongue-twisting name ethylenediamine tetraacetic acid (we'll save lots of space and tongue-twisting by calling it EDTA). The EDTA molecule also has an ethylene bridge and two amine groups, but with the difference that the hydrogen atoms of the amine groups have been replaced by acetic acid groups (—CH₂COOH);

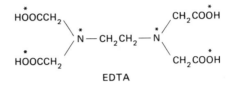

EDTA

Once again, the coordinating sites (electron-pair donor atoms) have been marked by stars. The EDTA molecule, as you can see, has six coordinating sites.

EDTA has found wide use in the removal of iron from public water supplies. Many fresh water sources contain enough dissolved salts of iron to be a problem. When water containing iron stands for any period of time, a sediment forms. Stains often develop in sinks and in the family laundry. Upon occasion even the flavor of food can be adversely affected. Many communities have had this problem. Unfortunately, until EDTA became available, there was very little anyone could do about it. Without chelation, iron is almost impossible to remove economically.

Chelation by EDTA, however, solves the problem. When it is added to the water supply, the iron ions are immediately sequestered, or bound up. They become so tightly bound they can't be detected even by very sensitive chemical tests. For all practical purposes, the iron behaves as if it had disappeared completely. EDTA chelated iron (FeEDTA⁻) forms as follows. When an EDTA molecule is added to the water, each of the four —CH₂COOH groups loses a hydrogen ion (a positively charged hydrogen atom, H^+):

$$-CH_2COOH \rightarrow -CH_2COO^- + H^+$$

Now, in addition to the two nitrogen atoms, four negatively charged oxygen atoms are available as electron-pair donors. Iron ions usually occur in water solutions in the triply charged form (Fe^{3+}). Thus, the negatively charged oxygen ends of the —CH₂COO⁻ groups and the negatively charged nitrogen atoms of the substituted amine groups converge on the Fe^{3+} ion and trap it. Five rings are formed (Figure 4-5), and the molecule as a whole carries a charge of minus one because there are four negative $-CH_2COO^-$ groups to each Fe^{3+} ion.

Figure 4-5. The five-ring structure of EDTA-chelated iron.

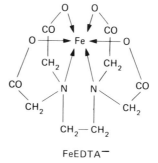

FeEDTA$^-$

Chelates and Food

Chelates have also turned out to be useful for preserving foods. Many foods contain traces of metals. Some of these trace metals can have serious adverse effects on the color of a food, its purity, and its stability. Often the undesirable effects occur as solids settling out, or rapid air oxidation leading to spoilage.

In some foods, only one part per million (ppm) of a metallic ion will stimulate air oxidation. This is what you are looking at when cut apples turn brown and green vegetables spoil. Traces of metal also cause rancidity in fats and oils, and the chemical destruction of some vitamins. Quite clearly these effects could be prevented if the chemical influence of the trace metals could be eliminated.

For a chelate to do this, however, it would have to have an extremely low toxicity, as well as the ability to sequester the objectionable ions. The calcium chelate of disodium ethylenediamine tetraacetic acid is one of a number of compounds that seem to fill the bill. See Figure 4-6. This molecule has sodium atoms substituted for the terminal hydrogen atoms on two of the $-CH_2COOH$ groups. These two groups therefore cannot sequester metallic ions. In addition, this substance is already a chelate; the disodium EDTA molecule has reacted with and bound up a calcium ion. The molecule is neutral because the calcium ion has a charge of plus two, and there were two —CH₂COO⁻ groups available for bonding. As the diagram indicates, the calcium ion is held by four bonds, and there are three rings.

Figure 4-6.   The calcium chelate of   disodium   ethylenediamine tetraacetic acid.

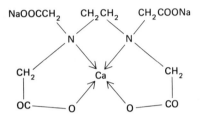

At this point you may be asking yourself how a substance that is already a chelate can trap metallic ions. The answer lies in what the chemist calls the metal-chelate replacement series. First, however, consider what happens when a piece of copper metal is immersed in a solution of silver nitrate. The copper replaces the silver from solution. Copper ions go into solution and silver metal plates out on the piece of copper. You might want to cut the piece of copper in the shape of a Christmas tree and do this demonstration just before the holidays. In a bright spotlight the tiny crystals of silver are quite beautiful as they accumulate.

The metal-chelate replacement series is similar to the metal replacement series suggested by the copper-silver ion reaction. In the metal-chelate replacement series, the chelates are arranged in the order of increasing stability.

Calcium chelates have the lowest stability of the chelates commonly formed from the metals found in foods. If some calcium EDTA is added to a food containing traces of an objectionable metal, there will be a choice between two possible chelates; that of the undesirable metal or that of the calcium EDTA. Since physical systems almost always move in the direction of the lowest possible energy content, the calcium ions will be replaced from the EDTA by the other metallic ions. This frees calcium ions in the foodstuff, but sequesters the objectionable ions, preventing them from causing color changes, air oxidation, or what have you.

Fortunately for food chemists, calcium EDTA has an extremely low toxicity. Thus it may be used in foods without fear of side effects in the ultimate consumer of the food.

Chelates and Chemical Analysis

Analytic chemists, those dedicated souls who make the detection of one or two atoms per million atoms a commonplace thing, have also found important uses for chelates. For example, it is very often necessary to analyze hard water. In this analysis the chemist wants to know the total hardness of the water, that is, the exact concentration of calcium and magnesium ions. These ions occur in very small quantities, requiring a high degree of precision in the analytic work. EDTA is used for the analysis of hard water. When a known volume of EDTA of known concentration is added to the water sample until all of the calcium and magnesium ions have reacted, it is a simple matter to calculate the concentrations of the ions in the sample. The endpoint of the reaction, that is, the point at which all of the ions have reacted, is usually marked by an indicator. Most indicators change color quite dramatically at the endpoint of a reaction. The chemist simply adds his known reagent until the color change occurs, and then uses the data to make his calculations.

Some chelating agents form highly colored compounds with metallic ions. Thus they become the basis of a somewhat different scheme of analysis—*colorimetric* analysis. The color of a compound can be used two ways in analytic work. First, the appearance of a characteristic color shows the presence of a given substance—it tells the chemist "what" is there. Second, the intensity of the color can be compared to a set of standard colors—each intensity corresponding to a specific concentration—telling the chemist "how much" of a substance is present. Today quantitative analysis by visual colorimetry (comparison using the eyes) is on the way out because very sensitive photometric instruments have been developed. In these instruments a photoelectric cell replaces the eye, making the evaluation of color intensity a far more exact science.

The chemist still uses his eyes, however, for qualitative identification of metal-chelate complexes. The use of dimethylglyoxime,

$$CH_3-C = NOH$$
$$CH_3-\overset{|}{C} = NOH$$

for the identification of the Ni^{2+} ion is a good example. When this compound is added to a solution containing Ni^{2+} ions, a deeply colored scarlet red chelate forms and settles out. See Figure 4-7.

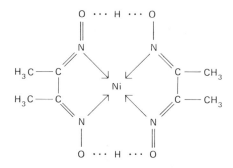

Figure 4-7.   Structure of the scarlet colored chelate formed in the identification of Ni^{2+} ion using dimethylglyoxime.

This compound is highly insoluble in water. It not only is a means of detecting the presence of nickel ion in solution, it may also be used as a reagent for separating nickel from a mixture of metallic ions. The dimethylglyoxime bonds with nickel ions to the total exclusion of other ions in the system.

Chelates in Nature

While man has made enormous strides in the past three decades with chelates, he must still take a back seat to nature in their utilization. Two of the most important compounds found in living things are chelates —chlorophyll and hemoglobin. Moreover, the chelate portion of the molecules of these substances is identical. Figure 4-8 shows the porphyrin ring, a flat arrangement with four nitrogen atoms at the corners of a central square.

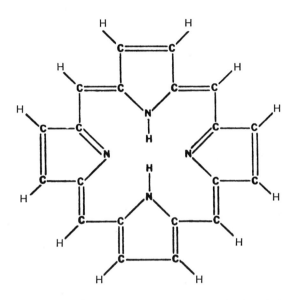

Figure 4-8.   The porphyrin ring. This structure is the chelate portion of both the chlorophyll and the hemoglobin molecules.

In chlorophyll the chelated metal is magnesium. It is bonded to the four central nitrogen atoms of the porphyrin ring. In hemin, the oxidized form of hemoglobin, the chelated metal is iron (See Figure 4-9).

Other compounds found in living tissues that serve as chelating agents are the cytochromes (oxidative enzymes), and citric, lactic, and tartaric acids. These acids prevent the precipitation of metallic ions in body fluids. Even the soil contains chelating agents—these hold iron and calcium, making them available for absorption by plants.

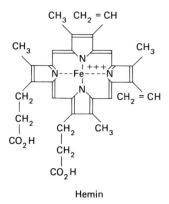

Figure 4-9. The structure of hemin, the oxidized form of hemoglobin. In this molecule the porphyrin ring sequesters an iron ion.

Hemin

Chelation, a relatively new tool of the chemist, holds unlimited possibilities for the future. In addition to the many uses described in this chapter, it has found use in the decontamination of radioactive deposits, as a rust and scale remover, in sequestering trace metals that discolor dyes, and in the removal of iron stains from fabrics.

Chelating agents have also been used as antioxidants in rubber, as antijelling agents in fuel oils, and antigumming agents in gasoline. They have even found use in biology and medicine—as plant growth regulators, antioxidants in drugs, and in the prevention of allergic reactions to metallic ions.

5

ION EXCHANGE – "Horse Trading" at the Molecular Level

Bartering has always been one of man's most cherished arts. From prehistoric man, who may have acquired a sharpened stone in exchange for a joint of fresh meat, to today's little boy, who gives up a prized pet turtle for a rusty jackknife, the participants in a mutually agreeable trade always come away from the transaction with a sense of satisfaction.

Trading, it would seem, is here to stay. Thus, even scientists who confine their trading to the humdrum business activities needed to get along from day to day can become very excited when they discover a new kind of trading. Imagine the interest and curiosity that must have gripped the first man to discover that certain molecules are capable of exchanging one kind of atom for another.

This process, called *ion exchange,* was first observed during the mid-nineteenth century. These first investigators were studying the power of soil to hold water-soluble fertilizers, even in a heavy rain. In the earliest experiments a mixture of soil and ammonium sulfate, $(NH_4)_2SO_4$, was placed in a glass tube, and water was poured through the tube. The effluent (the water solution coming out the bottom of the tube—see the diagram below) was then analyzed. It turned out to contain quite large amounts of calcium sulfate, $CaSO_4$, but little or no ammonia or ammonium compounds.

In another experiment similar to this one, a solution of potassium chloride, KCl, was slowly trickled through a column of soil. When the effluent was analyzed, it showed sodium ions, Na^+, and calcium ions, Ca^{2+}, but far fewer potassium ions, K^+. See Figure 5-1. Apparently some substance in the soil had taken up some of the K^+ ions, releasing an equivalent number of Na^+ and Ca^{2+} ions.

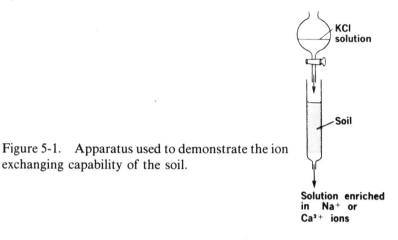

Figure 5-1.   Apparatus used to demonstrate the ion exchanging capability of the soil.

Today we know that the ion exchangers in the soil are acid substances found in minerals and clay, as well as compounds produced by the decay of soil vegetation.

Ions and Electrostatic Attraction

To get at a molecular explanation of ion exchange, we'll have to backtrack a bit. If you recall, ionic compounds consist of oppositely charged particles, ions, held together by electrostatic attraction. Sodium chloride, NaCl, the compound we discussed in Chapter One, is a good example. Under ordinary circumstances the positive and negative ions in an ionic compound are bound so tightly it is very difficult to separate them. In those compounds that have the property of ion exchange, however, it is possible to substitute for the bound ions, thus releasing them. Generally speaking, an ion will displace another from an ion exchanger if it is bound up more tightly than the ion being substituted for.

The first synthetic ion exchanger was produced in Germany in 1858. Eichhorn, its creator, used knowledge gained by studying the ion exchanging properties of the soil to put together the proper ingredients. He mixed sodium silicate and sodium aluminate solutions, getting a white jellylike substance. When this material was dried and crushed, it made a fine ion exchanger. Curiously enough, this first synthetic ion exchanger is still one of the most important commercial exchangers. It is widely used for softening water.

Most of the ion exchangers in use today are made up of very large molecules, linked together in a complex network. Basically, the main part of these giant molecules is a multiply-charged ion. Neutrality is maintained by many smaller ions of opposite charge, loosely held by electrostatic attraction. It is these smaller ions that trade places with the ions in a solution percolating down through the exchanger.

In slightly different terms, ion exchangers can be thought of as insoluble acids or bases capable of forming insoluble salts. This insolubility in water is important, for the exchanger would be of little use if it dissolved in the solution undergoing ion exchange. The cross-linked molecular network of modern exchangers may swell in water, but the molecular links throughout the network prevent dissolving in water or other solutions.

Thus, for a solid ion exchanger to work, it must have three characteristics. First, it must contain many ions held loosely enough to be easily removed. Second, it must be insoluble in water and in the solutions percolated through the exchanger. Third, there must be sufficient open space within the network of molecules for smaller ions to move in and out freely.

Since the molecules in an ion exchange compound may be either acidic or basic, two types of exchangers may be identified. The first are called *cation-exchangers.* Cations are positive ions, hence cation-exchangers will remove positive ions from solutions. Cation-exchange compounds contain acidic groups, such as carboxyl (—COOH) and sulfonic acid (—SO_3H) groups, at regular intervals along the carbon chains of the molecular network. Figure 5-2 shows a portion of the network of a sulfonic acid type cation-exchanger. Note how the molecular chains are cross-linked. The structural formula of a short piece of the molecular chain is drawn beneath the schematic diagram.

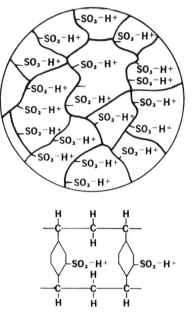

Figure 5-2. A portion of the molecular network of a cation-exchanger. Such exchangers remove positive ions from solutions.

The second type of ion exchange compounds are the *anion-exchangers*. Anions are negatively charged, hence anion-exchangers will remove negative ions from solutions. Anion-exchange compounds contain basic groups, such as the strongly basic group $-N(CH_3)_3OH$, or the weakly basic groups $-NH_2$ and $-N(CH_3)_2$. In the case of the strongly basic group $-N(CH_3)_3OH$, the $-OH$ groups are replaceable, putting OH⁻ ions in solution. The molecular network for a strongly basic ion exchanger, along with the structural formula for a portion of the chain is shown in Figure 5-3.

Let's look into two simple experiments to get at the heart of the matter; how ion exchange reactions take place. Suppose we set up the apparatus shown in Figure 5-4. The lefthand tube is packed with a cation-exchanger; the righthand tube contains an anion-exchanger. Above each tube we suspend a separatory funnel, and below them beakers to catch the effluent solutions. Both separatory funnels contain sodium chloride (NaCl) solution.

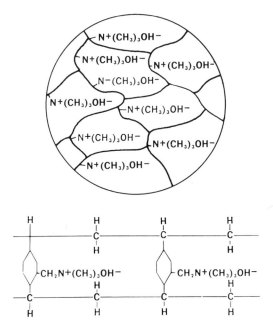

Figure 5-3. A portion of the molecular network of an anion-exchanger. Such exchangers remove negative ions from solutions.

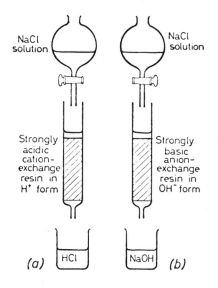

Figure 5-4. Apparatus used to demonstrate how ion-exchange reactions occur.

To simplify matters we represent the cation-exchanging compound in funnel (a) by H-R. R stands for the insoluble molecular network, and H represents exchangeable hydrogen ions. We say the exchanger is in the H^+ form. Now, if a solution of sodium chloride is allowed to seep slowly downward through the exchanger, the following reaction takes place.

$$H-R + NaCl \longrightarrow Na-R + HCl$$

Sodium ions diffuse throughout the molecular network, coming into intimate contact with the many hydrogen ions attached to the exchanger. The sodium ions then replace the hydrogen ions. The result is an effluent solution of hydrogen chloride (hydrochloric acid), rather than the original solution, sodium chloride. The amount of exchange that takes place depends mainly on two factors; (1) the relative attractive strength of the hydrogen and sodium ions for the molecular network, and (2) the amount of sodium chloride in the original solution.

In the second experiment the NaCl solution is percolated through a strongly basic anion-exchanger. In this case, the reaction is

$$R-OH + NaCl \longrightarrow R-Cl + NaOH$$

Thus, we see that the sodium ions have replaced the hydroxide ions (OH^-), leaving the exchanger in the chloride form. In the first experiment, the exchanger came out in the sodium form.

Most exchangers can be regenerated. In the examples above, if we poured hydrochloric acid through column (a) and sodium hydroxide solution through column (b) the compounds would be restored to their original condition.

Deionizing Water

What we have just described is the basis for a relatively new way to produce "distilled" water without the time and trouble involved in actual distillation. All that is necessary is to pass the impure water through a cation-exchanger and an anion-exchanger in succession. Of course, ion-exchange removes ions from the impure (or tap) water, but not organic substances.

During World War II torpedoed seamen and fliers downed in the ocean relied on compact little ion exchangers for drinking water. These emergency deionizing systems did a very passable job of converting seawater for drinking. Each kit consisted of a plastic bag and six candy-bar-sized wafers. The wafers contained a high capacity cation-exchanger, with silver ion as the replaceable ion. A pint of seawater plus one of the wafers was placed in the plastic sack and kneaded to speed up the circulation of the ions. The exchanger took the sodium and magnesium ions from the seawater, releasing silver ions in their place.

$$Ag-R + Na^+ \longrightarrow Na-R + Ag^+$$
$$2Ag-R + Mg^{2+} \longrightarrow R-Mg-R + 2Ag^+$$

But then the silver ions reacted with the chloride ions of the seawater, producing the insoluble compound silver chloride.

$$Ag^+ + Cl^- \longrightarrow AgCl$$

After straining out the solids by means of a canvas filter, the men could safely drink the water.

Several different types of reactions can be carried out by ion exchange. In general, the types of reactions possible depend upon the types of exchangers available. Let's look at the reaction possibilities for *strongly acidic exchangers* and for *strongly basic exchangers.*

Strongly acidic exchangers contain strong acid groups, such as the $-SO_3H$ group. These exchangers can be used to neutralize or absorb bases. This reaction is analogous to the familiar acid-base reaction of solution chemistry. In solution chemistry a salt plus water is produced:

$$\text{Acid} + \text{Base} \longrightarrow \text{Salt} + \text{Water}$$

When an ion exchanger is substituted for the acid, water is still produced, but the salt is insoluble. The acidic exchanger has been converted to the salt form, metallic ions having taken the place of the hydrogen ions in the exchanger:

$$R-SO_3H + NaOH \rightarrow R-SO_3Na + H_2O$$

If enough of the ion-exchange compound is used, all of the base will be absorbed. Thus, this is a good method for removing a caustic base from solution.

Base exchange reactions in neutral or alkaline solutions are also possible. For example, suppose we wish to convert an exchanger in the potassium form to the sodium form. This is easily done by percolating a solution of sodium chloride through the column. The sodium ions will exchange with the potassium ions, yielding the exchanger in the sodium form and a solution of potassium chloride.

$$R-SO_3K + NaCl \rightarrow R-SO_3Na + KCl$$

Similarly, we can convert an exchanger in the sodium form into the potassium form by passing a solution of potassium hydroxide through the column.

$$R-SO_3Na + KOH \rightarrow R-SO_3K + NaOH$$

Another important property of strongly acidic exchangers is salt-splitting. In salt-splitting the ions of a strong-acid salt (e.g. NaCl, K_2SO_4) are separated.

$$R-SO_3H + NaCl \rightarrow R-SO_3Na + HCl$$

This is equivalent to the first step in the demineralization of water by ion exchange. In the second step a strongly basic exchanger would remove the chloride ions.

Strongly basic exchangers do just the opposite of strongly acidic exchangers. Basic exchangers, of course, contain basic groups such as the $-N(CH_3)_3OH$ group. As expected, they neutralize or absorb acids, once again producing water and an insoluble salt.

$$R-N(CH_3)_3OH + HCl \rightarrow R-N(CH_3)_3Cl + H_2O$$
$$R-N(CH_3)_3OH + CH_3COOH \rightarrow R-N(CH_3)_3OOCCH_3 + H_2O$$

They can also be used over a wide range of pH values for acid exchange reactions.

$$R-N(CH_3)_3Cl + NaNO_3 \rightarrow R-N(CH_3)_3NO_3 + NaCl$$

Finally, strongly basic exchangers will also split salts.

$$R-N(CH_3)_3OH + KCl \rightarrow R-N(CH_3)_3Cl + KOH$$

Probably the most interesting aspect of ion exchange is the wide number of applications that have developed in recent years. These applications can be divided into three general groups. The first includes all simple exchange reactions, that is, reactions in which ions in a solution are replaced by ions from the exchanger. These include the preparation of acids, bases, and salts, and the removal of salts from aqueous solutions.

Removing Radiostrontium from Milk

For example, a few years ago when it seemed very likely that continued atmospheric testing of nuclear weapons would contaminate milk with radioactive strontium, the Public Health Service, the Atomic Energy Commission, and the Department of Agriculture cooperatively developed an ion-exchange system to remove the radiostrontium from milk. The ion-exchanger contained exchangeable calcium ions. The process was capable of removing 98 percent of the radiostrontium without substantially changing the flavor characteristics of the milk. See Figure 5-5. Fortunately, with the cessation of atmospheric testing the radiostrontium content of milk has fallen off sharply. It may be that we will never have to treat milk to remove radioactive contaminants, but it is comforting to know that such processes are available.

The second type of application is ion-exchange chromatography. Chromatography is the separation and identification of substances by means of color. Ion-exchange chromatography is useful for separating a mixture of closely related ions. Thus, when a solution containing such a mixture is percolated through the proper exchanger, the concentrations of the different ions and their relative affinities for the exchanger

Figure 5-5.   Pilot plant of an ion-exchange system used to remove radi-ostrontium from milk. This plant processes 100 gallons of milk an hour. (Photo courtesy of U.S. Department of Agriculture)

will determine their rates of exchange. Since these rates will differ, the result is a separation of the ions into distinct bands as the solution seeps down through the column. Finally, if the different ions can be colored in some way, they can be identified as they separate into bands.

The best known application of ion-exchange chromatography is the separation of the lanthanide elements, a group of elements whose prop-erties are so similar they defy separation by "wet chemistry" methods. Other applications have appeared from time to time also. For example, just a few years ago ion-exchange chromatography was used to discover a new element, mendelevium. In the crucial experiment, just two atoms of mendelevium were separated by ion exchange, and then identified by a series of predicted radioactive reactions. An extraordinary feat by anyone's standards!

Catalysts and Fuel Cells

Since ion-exchange substances are essentially insoluble acids or bases, they can be used as catalysts. Catalysts, as you recall, are substances that speed up reactions without entering into the reactions themselves. Many organic reactions are catalyzed by acids or bases, accounting for the fairly wide use of ion-exchangers for this purpose. A distinct advantage is that the solid exchanger can be removed from the reaction chamber with little or no difficulty, making isolation of the reaction products a much simpler matter.

A third and final application worth mentioning is the ion-exchange fuel cell. Fuel cells are devices that convert the energy of a burning fuel directly into electricity. Thus, instead of the heat and light expected from the combustion of a fuel, a flow of electrons (an electric current) is produced.

In the ion-exchange membrane cell the fuel is hydrogen. As Figure 5-6 shows, the cell consists of an outer container, two gas chambers, two catalytic electrodes, and the ion-exchange membrane—the electrolyte that transports ions from one electrode to the other.

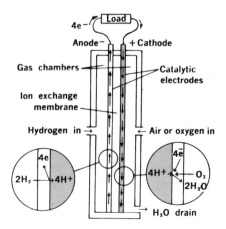

Figure 5-6.   Diagram of an ion-exchange fuel cell. The fuel is hydrogen; the ion-exchange electrolyte is at the center.

The ion-exchange electrolyte is what we might call a quasi solid. It consists of the familiar three-dimensional molecular network, but in this case it contains water bound up in the interstitial spaces of the network in addition to the active ion-exchange groups. In this cell the ion-exchange groups are sulfonic acid groups, $—SO_3H$. Just as an acid solution conducts electricity, this membrane conducts by means of the migration of hydrogen ions.

The process is really quite simple. Hydrogen gas enters at the left and reacts at the porous anode, producing electrons and hydrogen ions. The H^+ ions migrate through the membrane to the cathode, where they react with oxygen (fed in at the right) and with the electrons, which

Figure 5-7.   The prototype ion-exchange fuel cell. Starting with hydrogen as the fuel, the electricity generated spins the miniature propeller. Ion-exchange fuel cells were later used in the Gemini manned space flights. (Photo courtesy of GE Research and Development Center)

have migrated through the external circuit (the load). This external-circuit current can be used for any number of direct current requirements—within the energy limits of the cell, of course. The overall reaction is simply the burning of hydrogen in air or oxygen to produce water. Thus, the cell converts chemical energy directly into electrical energy.

Let's look at the reactions. If we write down the anode and cathode reactions as follows, and then add them up, we see that they do indeed come out to be just the burning of hydrogen.

$$\text{Anode:} \quad 2H_2 \rightarrow 4H^+ + 4e^-$$

$$\text{Cathode:} \quad 4e^- + 4H^+ + O_2 \rightarrow 2H_2O$$

$$\text{Overall:} \quad 2H_2 + O_2 \rightarrow 2H_2O$$

Ion-exchange fuel cells have shown great promise for a variety of ground, space, and undersea uses. Their size is also an advantage—they are flat, thus many of them can be assembled side by side without taking up too much room.

6

PHOTOCHROMIC GLASS – Color and Shadow in Optical Glass

Walk into almost any optometrist's office, and you'll probably find one or two green plants decorating the premises. While the plants sit quietly in the sun, absorbing its energy, the optometrist may be on the other side of the room fitting a rather special pair of eyeglasses to a person's head. Having adjusted the glasses so that they fit correctly, the optometrist suggests to his customer that he walk over into the sunlight to test how they work. The customer gets up, checks his appearance in a mirror to note the clarity of the lenses in the eyeglasses, and walks over to the window. Just as soon as the sunlight strikes the lenses, they begin to darken! Within a few minutes the eyeglasses look more like gray colored sunglasses than the clear eyeglasses they were before being exposed to the sun. The customer then returns to the darker side of the room and notes with satisfaction that the lenses are clearing. Before too long they are very nearly as clear as they were before the little experiment.

Photochemical Reactions

Instant sunglasses! Believe it or not, they really exist. You can probably purchase a set for yourself in your own home town. But why mention green plants in connection with these unusual eyeglasses? The answer is simple. A *photochemical* reaction is taking place both within the leaves of the plant and within the optical glass. In most chemical reactions the particles absorb enough energy to react by means of high-speed collisions; these collisions are the result of the thermal motion of the particles. Not so in photochemical reactions, in which the

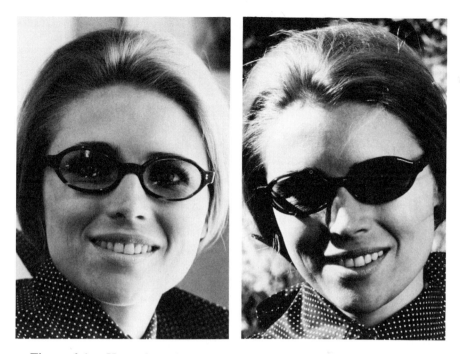

Figure 6-1. How photochromic eyeglass lenses work. Indoors and at night, her glasses are clear. Outdoors during the daylight hours the lenses darken. (Photo courtesy of Corning Glass Works)

energy needed to produce reaction is the energy of the absorbed light. In the green plant the photochemical reaction is photosynthesis, in which carbon dioxide is absorbed from the atmosphere and carbohydrate is produced. In the eyeglass lenses, reactive particles embedded in the glass absorb light energy and react to produce a substance that causes darkening by absorbing and reflecting some of the light that passes through the lens. Then, when the intensity of the incident light decreases, the reaction reverses and the glass clears.

This unusual chemical behavior under the influence of light is the result of incorporating submicroscopic silver halide (from *halogen*— chlorine, bromine, iodine, etc.) particles in the optical glass. This type of glass is called *photochromic glass.* The discovery that silver halides precipitated in glass react reversibly under light goes back some eight to ten years. This discovery was made by scientists who were investigating the completely disordered molecular structure of glass. As part of this research, efforts were made to induce the beginnings of order among the molecules of glass. This region is a sort of submicroscopic "no man's land." It lies between the appearance of true crystals down to the point where the particles are so small they probably contain too few atoms to form a crystal. No one knows whether this region contains true crystals, or even if the particles actually are crystals but are just too small to be identified.

In any event, this is the structural region in the glass in which the silver halides are deposited. Now, silver halides are the light-sensitive substances embedded in the emulsion on photographic film. When a piece of unexposed film is exposed to light, the silver halides absorb light energy. This initiates decomposition of the halides, but the reaction does not proceed in the dry state. As you well know, the film must be immersed in a chemical developer to complete the decomposition of the silver halides. When this is done, the reaction produces finely divided silver:

$$n\text{AgCl} \xrightarrow{\text{light}} n\text{Ag} + n\text{Cl}$$

The silver atoms thus precipitated then come together to form the familiar dark part of the negative.

$$n\text{Ag} \longrightarrow (\text{Ag})_n$$

How dark, that is, how opaque the finely divided silver is on the negative depends on the amount of light reflected to the film by the various objects that were photographed. The negative image of a white shirt is quite dark because a great deal of light is reflected from the shirt. Conversely, on a negative the image of a dark jacket is light (less opaque) because less light is reflected from the jacket. When the print (or positive) is made from the negative, light passes through the negative to the emulsion on the surface of the printing paper. More light passes through the less opaque areas of the negative and less light through the more opaque areas. Thus, the print develops with the white shirt light and the dark jacket dark.

While silver halides are used in both photographic emulsions and photochromic glass, there is an important fundamental difference. The photodecomposition reaction of the silver halides in a photographic emulsion is irreversible. Once film has been exposed, the reaction cannot be reversed, as many photographers have discovered to their dismay with their first double exposure.

Photochromic Reaction in Glass Reversible

The photodecomposition reaction in the photochromic glass, however, is reversible. When light strikes the glass, the silver halides decompose, depositing finely divided silver. The glass then darkens as the silver particles absorb light. But, when the light has been removed, the glass quickly clears to its original state—the silver atoms have recombined with the halogen atoms to form once again the nonabsorbing silver halide compound.

Perhaps the most exciting aspect of this phenomenon is that the reversible reaction will continue indefinitely with no loss of activity. The chemist would say that there is no tendency for the system to *photodegrade;* that is, no decomposition products build up to destroy the chemical activity of the silver halides. In one test during the development of photochromic glass, a sample of the glass showed no fatigue in darkening or clearing behavior after more than two years of continuous outdoor exposure. Many researchers feel that this type of photochromic glass is the only one capable of remaining permanently active.

As mentioned, the unique behavior of silver halides in glass was first discovered by researchers studying the basic structure of glass. In particular, the scientists were interested in what happened to various substances dissolved in molten glass as the glass was allowed to harden. Molten glass, or silica, is an extremely viscous, or syrupy, liquid. It is a three-dimensional substance whose basic structure is a network of interconnected silicon dioxide molecules. These molecules are assembled in the form of the now familiar silicon-oxygen tetrahedron (Figure 6-2).

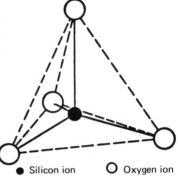

Figure 6-2. Glass is a three-dimensional network of interconnected silicon dioxide molecules, arranged in tetrahedral form.

● Silicon ion   ○ Oxygen ion

The tetrahedral units are then joined together by oxygen bonds in a random manner. In the molten state, these chemical bonds are continually breaking and reforming. This is illustrated in Figure 6-3 by showing the units in a regular array (a), and then by showing them disordered (b) following the breaking and reforming of bonds.

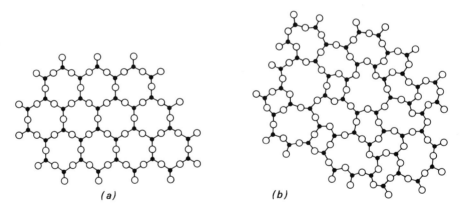

(a)   *(b)*

Figure 6-3.   The regular array of silicon-oxygen tetrahedra in solid glass (*a*) becomes disordered in the molten state (*b*) when the bonds between the atoms break and reform in a random manner.

Molten silica is a powerful universal solvent. The atoms of practically every element can be incorporated into its structure. While some atoms can become part of the structural network, most become an ionic plasma moving through holes in the network. In Figure 6-4, sodium ions are shown moving through the openings in the constantly changing network structure.

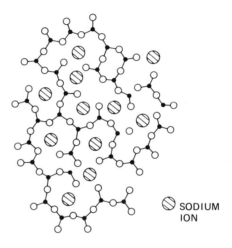

Figure 6-4. Sodium ions in motion within the openings of the structural network of molten glass.

SODIUM ION

At high temperatures we can picture these sodium ions as fish swimming through a three-dimensional net whose meshes become gradually more rigid and smaller in size as the material cools. Put another way, at the high temperatures of molten glass, the ions of dissolved solutes are free to move about. Then, as the molten glass cools, the network becomes more and more rigid, until it is completely solid. Solidification usually takes place between 400°C and 600°C. The solute ions, however, usually do not "freeze" at the same high temperature as the glass network. Thus, at temperatures at which the glass is completely rigid, diffusion and chemical reaction can still take place among the solute ions. At even lower temperatures, but still above room temperature, the solute ions also "freeze" in place; translational motion by diffusion no longer takes place. Thus, at room temperatures the ions are locked in place. This shows that reactions that occur upon the absorption of high-energy radiation (light) are the result of electron shifting and not molecular rearrangement.

In photochromic glass, the solute ions are silver (Ag^+) and halide (primarily Cl^-) ions. These ions, called microcrystals, are embedded in the holes of the chemically inert glass network. Studies indicate that there are about 8×10^{15} silver halide crystals per cubic centimeter of the photochromic glass. More important, the diameter of the individual crystals is about 50 Å (one angstrom is 10^{-8} cm), and the crystals are about 500 Å apart. Very likely the small size of the crystals plus the relatively large distance between them is the reason that photodecomposition of the silver halides is reversible. As one chemist put it, ". . . the photolytic color centers cannot diffuse away, or grow into stable silver particles, or react chemically to produce an irreversible decomposition of silver halide."

Types of Reactions

The reactions that take place in photochromic glass consist of three processes—*optical darkening, optical bleaching,* and *thermal bleaching.* In optical darkening, incident light darkens the glass, and the removal of light will cause it to clear. In the case of silver chloride glasses that are darkened by only ultraviolet wavelengths, exposure to longer-wave visible and near-infrared radiation within the absorption band of the glass's color centers results in an accelerated clearing. This is optical bleaching. Glasses of this type fade more rapidly in visible light than in the dark. Application of heat also produces clearing—this is thermal bleaching.

If the photochromic glass contains silver chloride, these reactions may be represented as follows:

$$AgCl \underset{\text{heat}}{\overset{\text{light}}{\rightleftharpoons}} Ag^0 + Cl^0$$

But suppose we expose a silver chloride glass to ultraviolet and visible light at the same time? As you might expect, such a glass does not darken as much as it would if exposed to ultraviolet light alone.

Glasses containing mixtures of metals have also been produced. For example, the reactions that take place in a glass containing a mixture of silver ion (Ag^+) and cuprous ion (Cu^+) would be as follows:

$$Ag^+ + Cu^+ \underset{\text{heat}}{\overset{\text{light}}{\rightleftharpoons}} Ag^0 + Cu^{2+}$$

Regardless of the composition of the microcrystals embedded in the glass, however, the reactions are reversible because the light-absorbing particles are not free to move about and clump together into a mass of metal. The rigid framework of the glass structure holds them in place, separated at a distance of about 500 Å. As a result, the absorption of light produces only a darkening of the glass, rather than the opacity that would be produced if the silver atoms could come together into a large mass.

Writing with Light

A recent example of the use of photochromic glass is shown in Figure 6-5. This photo shows a computer terminal with a large display screen

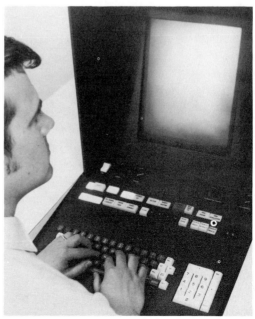

Figure 6-5. The keyboard and display screen of a computer terminal that uses photo-chromic glass to form images for display. (Photo courtesy of Corning Glass Works)

—as opposed to the usual paper printout. Consider a piece of paper and a pencil. When something is written or drawn on the paper with the pencil, that information is stored and displayed on the paper. It will stay there—available for reading—until erased.

Now consider a piece of photochromic glass and beams of "writing" and "erasing" light. The writing beam is ultraviolet light, which darkens the glass; the erasing beam is red, which causes the glass to clear. In the terminal shown in Figure 6-5, the photochromic glass is part of an electronic tube that generates the writing by means of beams of ultraviolet light. A flash of red light then "erases" the image, and the display screen is ready for the next assignment.

7

LIQUID CRYSTALS — A "Middle of the Road" Type of Matter

Strange as it may seem, all of the following tasks and devices have one thing in common—liquid crystals. The tasks are:

—measuring temperature variation by means of color change
—detecting structural flaws in opaque materials
—locating veins, arteries, or other anatomical structures beneath the skin
—detecting traces of chemical vapors in the atmosphere

Now how about some very new and unusual devices?

—colorful signs that turn on and off by means of an electric field
—a window that goes from cloudy to transparent and back again at the flick of a switch
—a television set the thickness of a picture frame

If this list of tasks and devices had been placed before you with no advanced warning, you would surely have said that there is no connection at all between them. But there is a connection. All of the tasks and all of the devices have at their roots that interesting but relatively little known form of matter—*liquid crystals.*

A Contradiction in Terms?

What are liquid crystals? A close look at the term *liquid crystal* seems to lead us into trouble. After all, liquids and crystals are quite different forms of matter; they have nothing in common. Or do they? Think back a moment to when you learned about the forms of matter. A liquid, you recall, is described as a free-flowing substance that takes the shape of its container. A crystal (i.e., a solid), on the other hand, is a rigid state of matter consisting of regularly spaced particles in a three-dimensional matrix. The particles in a liquid, of course, are arranged pretty much at random. In addition, because of the relatively low forces between them, the particles in a liquid flow around and over each other quite easily. The particles in a solid do not do this, for they are held in place by forces within the solid.

Thus solids seem to be the opposite of liquids. But surprisingly, there is a range of overlap. Liquid crystals fall in this range. They are substances that flow, pour, and take the shape of any container they are poured into. But their particles—their molecules—do something we ordinarily think of only in connection with solids. These molecules tend to form *within the liquid state* loosely ordered three-dimensional arrays rather like the lattice structure of a solid crystalline substance.

Mechanically, liquid crystals resemble high viscosity liquids over a range from honey all the way to "solid" glass, which is really a liquid in the solid state. Optically, however, they exhibit properties usually associated only with crystalline solids. They scatter light in symmetrical patterns, and reflect different colors depending on the viewing angle. This is called *anisotropy*. Evidence such as this tells us that the liquid-crystal state is a liquid form of matter with an internal structure much like that of crystalline solids.

If matter is classified in terms of the degree of order among its particles, then gases and true liquids are in an *amorphous* state; the molecules are in a random array and move in a totally random manner. At the other end of the scale, the particles in a *crystalline* state are firmly fixed in a three-dimensional lattice. These particles move about also, but only within the region of their sites in the crystal lattice. In between the amorphous and the crystalline states we find the *mesomorphic* state, the region of liquid crystals. As pointed out, this is the region in which the properties of liquids and crystalline solids overlap.

Types of Liquid Crystals

There are three general types of liquid crystals; *smectic, nematic,* and *cholesteric.* As strange as these terms now look to you, they will become quite familiar once we have probed where they come from and what they mean. The first group of liquid crystals, named *smectic* from the Greek word for soap, is the most viscous and turbid, and contains oblong-shaped molecules arranged side by side in series of layers. The molecules within the layers are found to be arranged in two possible ways. They may be organized into regular lines and rows, or they may be randomly distributed. See Figure 7-1.

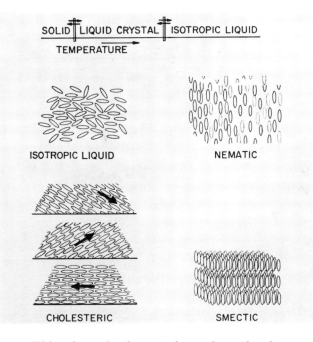

Figure 7-1.   This schematic diagram shows the molecular arrangement in an ordinary liquid, and in the three classes of liquid crystals—smectic, nematic, and cholesteric. The ordinary liquid is isotropic; that is, properties such as light scattering give the same results regardless of the axis along which they are measured. Liquid crystals are anisotropic; different values of the same properties are obtained when measured along different axes. (Art courtesy of RCA Laboratories)

In all smectic liquid crystals, the long axes of the molecules are arranged parallel to one another but perpendicular to the plane of the layer, which is just one molecule thick. These layers can slide back and forth over one another because the molecules are free to move from side to side or forward and backward, but not up and down. This occurs because the temperature of the substance is just high enough to break the bonds between the layers of molecules, but not high enough to break up the layers themselves.

An ordinary soap bubble is an example of a smectic liquid crystal. Soap molecules arranged side by side at the inner and outer edges of the soap film constitute the smectic layers. A simple aqueous solution of soap lies between the layers. This structure is shown in Figure 7-2.

Outer surface

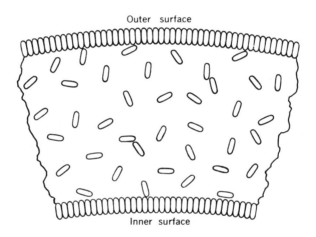

Inner surface

Figure 7-2.   The soap molecules at the inner and outer edges of the film of a soap bubble constitute a smectic liquid crystal.

The molecules are not drawn to scale; they are actually much smaller than shown here. An understanding of this structure, however, explains the ability of a soap bubble to expand and contract. Side-to-side attraction between the molecules in the inner and outer layers supplies the cohesive force that holds the bubble together. When the bubble expands, free soap molecules from the in-between soap solution are added to the smectic layers. As a result, the area of the soap film increases. When the bubble contracts, just the opposite occurs. Soap molecules move from the inner and outer layers into the soap solution, and the area of the film decreases.

Figure 7-3.   Photomicrograph of a smectic liquid crystal between two glass plates. X22. (Photo courtesy of Glenn H. Brown, Liquid Crystal Institute, Kent State University)

The second group of liquid crystals, named *nematic* from the Greek word for thread, exhibits a lower degree of order than smectic substances. Nematic substances are less viscous and more mobile than smectic liquid crystals. When a nematic liquid crystal is examined with a microscope, tiny threadlike structures appear. These structures seem to be the boundaries between regions of different molecular orientation.

Nematic liquid crystals contain rodlike organic molecules. These molecules are arranged with all of their long axes parallel, but they are not separated into layers. Figure 7-1 illustrates the structure of nematic liquid crystals. We can turn again to spaghetti for an analogy to the structure of nematic liquid crystals. Starting with the long package taken off the grocer's shelf, we somehow manage to break the long strands of spaghetti into many, many much shorter strands, each perhaps an inch or two long. In this condition, but still within the package, the pieces of spaghetti are free to roll around and slide back and forth and up and down, but they must remain parallel to the long axis of the package. While the molecules in a nematic liquid crystal are parallel to each other, they are not separated into layers. Thus, one way to think of a nematic liquid crystal is that it is a smectic material whose layers have penetrated each other.

The third class of liquid crystals was originally named *cholesteric* because its molecular structure is characteristic of a large number of compounds that derive from cholesterol. Cholesterol, as you probably know, is suspected of playing an important role in hardening of the arteries and heart disease. While cholesterol itself does not have a liquid-crystal phase, its molecular structure helps explain the unusual structure of cholesteric liquid crystals. In the diagram of the cholesterol molecule shown in Figure 7-4, you can see that the ring portion of the molecule is flat. The side chain of $-CH_3$ groups at the top right, however, extends upward from the plane of the rings.

Now let's look at the structure of a typical cholesteric liquid crystal. First, these substances resemble smectic liquid crystals in that the molecules are arranged in layers. The molecules within each layer, however, are parallel to each other, and thus resemble nematic liquid crystals. These molecular layers are very thin, with the long axes of the molecules parallel to the plane of the layers. As Figure 7-1 shows, the layers of molecules are rotated slightly relative to each other. This occurs because the side chains of CH_3 groups in the basic molecular group extend out of the molecular plane, and interfere with how the planes fit together. The net effect of this rotation is that the displaced planes trace out a helical pattern. Figure 7-1 shows in schematic form

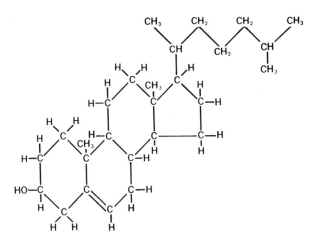

Figure 7-4. The structure of the cholesterol molecule. The side chain of -CH$_3$ groups at the top extends upward from the plane of the rings.

the layers, the orientation of the molecules within each layer, and the displacement from layer to layer. The displacement forces a given point on a molecule to trace out a helix. As you will see, it is this peculiarity of structure that accounts for many of the interesting properties of cholesteric liquid crystals.

The molecular structure of a cholesteric liquid crystal is very delicately balanced, and very easily disturbed. Thus small disturbances interfere with the weak forces between the molecules, and have the effect of slightly changing the molecular structure of the substance. But such a structural change also changes the optical properties of the liquid crystal.

Color Change and Molecular Twist

One of the most interesting optical properties of cholesteric liquid crystals is color variation with temperature change. Not long ago, it was discovered that these color changes are reversible, thus opening up whole new vistas for study and application.

Color change in cholesteric materials is a function of the amount of twist between the layers of the molecule. As the substance is heated or cooled, the degree of twist between the layers changes. But this also changes the energy states of the electrons within the molecule. Thus, different wavelengths are absorbed, and a different color is observed. Cholesteric derivatives can be compounded with temperature sensitivities from –20°C to 250°C, and with increments ranging from 3 to 50 degrees, depending upon the material.

These properties suggest many potential applications. In one such possibility, a cholesteric substance could be used to make a temperature profile of a part of the body. The hand, for example, could be painted with a suitable cholesteric mixture. If blood were then to be blocked by pressure, a temperature change in the veins would immediately show up as a color change in the liquid crystal. A lowering of the temperature of the fingertips can also be shown when cigarette smoke is inhaled. This occurs because the blood vessels dilate.

The color of cholesteric liquid crystals isn't dependent upon temperature alone. Both *chemical* and *mechanical* changes will bring about color changes. For example, very small amounts of certain chemical vapors will produce color changes in cholesteric substances. Two possibilities exist. If the liquid crystal reacts chemically with the vapor, the color change will be permanent. On the other hand, if the liquid crystal merely dissolves the chemical vapor, the color change will be reversible. Usually, only a few parts per million of the chemical vapor are needed to produce an immediate color change. The detection possibilities are obvious. For example, the unburned hydrocarbons usually found along with carbon monoxide could be detected, thus warning of carbon monoxide contamination.

Cholesteric compounds are also sensitive to changes in *shear,* a type of sliding distortion. Reaction to shear forces can be shown by mounting the liquid crystal between glass plates and then sliding, bending, or pressing the plates together. The shear forces applied produce a change in molecular structure, and hence a color change. *Pressure* and other mechanical stresses also affect the reflecting properties of cholesteric liquid crystals. These changes are less pronounced, however, than those induced by temperature and chemical influences.

Liquid Crystals and an Electric Field

Liquid crystals are also affected when they are subjected to an electric field. They may either become cloudy and translucent or change color, suggesting that they may find use in certain types of signs, or perhaps even in a television picture tube. There are two advantages to such devices. First, they reflect light instead of generating light. Thus, they can be viewed in full light without the image being "washed out" by the incident light. Second, since they do not emit light, they require very little power input, and should be inexpensive to operate.

Liquid crystals are affected by an electric field in two ways. First, since the liquid-crystal molecules are polar, the imposition of an electric field makes them line up. In a very real way, the molecules behave just as iron filings do in a magnetic field. They align themselves so that all of the positive ends of the molecules point in the same direction. At the same time, however, ionic impurities (both positively and negatively charged particles) are set in motion by the electric field. Positive ions move toward the negative electrode and negative ions move toward the positive electrode. Now, if the liquid-crystal molecules are oriented in such a direction that they obstruct the movement of the ions, a considerable amount of turbulence will be produced as the ions push through. This turbulence causes the liquid crystal, which was originally transparent, to become white or opaque. Just how this works is shown in Figure 7-5. In (a), a side view of a liquid crystal placed between glass plates is shown. Each plate has been coated with a transparent conducting material. An electric field has just been imposed upon the mixture of liquid-crystal molecules and ionic impurities. The device is transparent. In (b), however, the ions are moving toward the electrodes, disrupting the ordered state of the molecules as they do. This causes reflected or transmitted light to be scattered, and the device appears to be opaque. When the electric field is turned off, the molecules become locally reordered, the ions stop moving, and the fluid becomes clear once again.

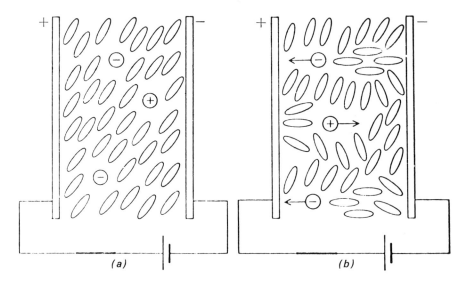

Figure 7-5.   How opacity is produced in a liquid-crystal display device. When an electric field is imposed upon the system, the moving ions disrupt the order of the liquid-crystal molecules, causing opacity.

If the conducting materials, that is, the electrodes on the glass plates, are put together so that they form figures or letters, the device becomes a sign when the electric field is turned on. On the other hand, if the entire surface is coated with the transparent electrode, it forms a window that can be clear or cloudy at the flick of a switch. Essentially the same principle applies for the proposed liquid-crystal television picture tube. The liquid-crystal material would be placed between the front and rear glass plates of the tube. The front glass plate would be coated with transparent electrodes, while the rear plate would be coated with reflecting electrodes. As usual, the circuitry of the set would lie behind the picture tube. Images would then be formed by having the liquid-crystal material scatter surrounding light. The electrodes on the rear plate would reflect light outward so that the moving images would be projected to the viewer. Many problems stand between this idea and its fulfillment. Without doubt, however, the many advantages of such a television tube will spur developmental research, and we will someday see a television set the thickness of a simple picture frame.

Figure 7-6.   In this liquid-crystal clock, the electrodes on the glass plates form the figures that give the time in hours and minutes. Such liquid-crystal display devices can now be used for print, still pictures, and moving images. (Photo courtesy of RCA Laboratories)

8

DETERGENTS – "Mr. Clean's" Dirty Trick

Just a few years ago a group of men in Sheboygan Falls, Wisconsin, stood in awe before an enormous bank of detergent foam. The mound of foam was about 25 feet deep, over a half-block long, and 75 feet wide. This foam, as snowy white as the fresh fall from a blizzard, was overflowing the Sheboygan River. It dwarfed the men, who could only look on in despair. There was no known way to combat this type of detergent foam.

At the same time, but on the East Coast, residents of Suffolk County, New York, never knew what would greet them when they turned on a faucet. Most of the time detergent foam gushed out with the water. What was happening was quite simple, although the solution to the problem was far from simple. Suffolk County is on Long Island, a land body surrounded on all four sides by seawater. For years its residents had been returning household waste water and sewage to the ground through septic tanks and cesspools. But the bulk of the freshwater supply for the county came from shallow wells. As you've probably already guessed, detergents were accumulating in the groundwater and polluting the freshwater supply.

Both these detergents and those at Sheboygan Falls were "hard" detergents; they resisted breakdown by biological action. Such nonbiodegradable detergents were in wide use until fairly recently. Then, in 1966, biodegradable detergents were substituted voluntarily by the nation's manufacturers of cleansers. Thus, the detergents in use today, while not completely degradable by the microorganisms in groundwater, are broken down sufficiently to reduce the foam problem to acceptable levels. Don't be misled, however, into believing that the detergent-foam problem has been solved. It hasn't, as even a casual look at one of our tidal streams or inland rivers fed by industry and household sewage will reveal. The foam may not be as dramatic, but it is still there. And curiously enough, it is involved in yet additional pollution problems. But more about this later.

Figure 8-1. Detergent foam in a stream. Just a few years ago this scene was repeated in many communities as nonbiodegradable detergents collected in the groundwater and polluted freshwater supplies. (Photo courtesy of U.S. Department of Agriculture)

Why Detergents?

At this point, you're probably wondering why we use detergents rather than good old-fashioned soap, which has been around for over 2000 years. Ask any housewife. She knows. Soaps are insoluble in hard water. They form insoluble precipitates with calcium, magnesium, and ferric ions. The result is the time-honored ring in the bath tub, or the scum at the bottom of the washing machine. Besides, modern detergents are much better cleansers than soap. Thus, the future may find us cleaner, but we may also be immersed in a veritable sea of foam.

The first detergent—that is, nonsoap with cleansing properties—was accidentally discovered in 1831 when a Frenchman named Edmond Fremy poured some sulfuric acid into olive oil. This produced a thick brown liquid, which Fremy dissolved in water. In a routine step even in 1831, he then neutralized the solution with caustic soda, and immediately observed that the mixture had a distinct soapy appearance. It could be made to foam (what would Fremy have done with his discovery if he could have foreseen the monumental problem this innocuous bit of foam was to become?), and when greasy objects were dipped into it, some of the grease was removed.

Fremy knew that he had come up with something unique—a substance made from an acid and oil that had cleansing properties—while soap itself was made by cooking an oil or fat with an alkali. Fremy was never able to separate the active ingredient in his mixture, so he never understood that he had produced the first sulfated oil, or true detergent.

Making Water Wetter

Today's detergents are referred to technically as *surfactants* (from surface-active agents) or *syndets* (from synthetic detergents). Both soaps and detergents behave in the same manner. They increase the *wetting action* of water by lowering its surface tension. Water by itself is a very poor cleansing agent, for its molecules are so polar they stick to each other through hydrogen bonds rather than penetrate into the nonpolar films of grease and oil that bind dirt particles to surfaces.

Soap molecules and detergent molecules are quite similar. In the formulas shown in Figure 8-2, note that both contain long hydrocarbon chains. This portion of the molecules is soluble in oils and greases, but not in water. At the ends of these hydrocarbon chains, however, there are quite different chemical groups. In the soap, this group makes the

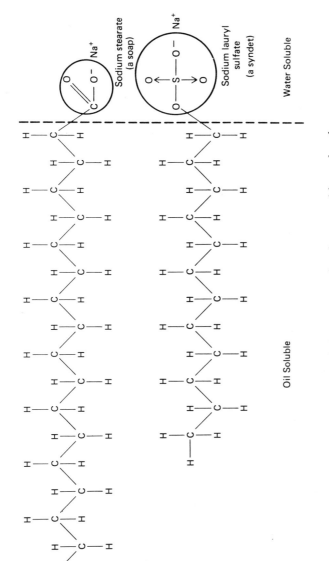

Figure 8-2. How soap and detergent molecules resemble each other. The difference between the two lies in the chemical group at the end of the hydrocarbon chain.

molecule the sodium (or potassium) salt of an organic acid. This end of the molecule is soluble in water. In a detergent, however, the water soluble group is much more complex, and as a result, more polar. It is this increased polarity that improves the "wettability" of detergents as compared to soaps.

Suppose, now, that we represent a detergent molecule as a small solid circle, the "head," with a straight "tail" protruding from the head. The head, of course, is the highly polar water soluble group, and the tail is the oil soluble hydrocarbon chain. See Figure 8-3.

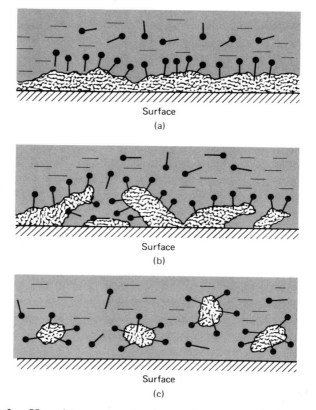

Figure 8-3.   How detergent molecules render grease soluble. See the text for details.

When a detergent is added to water and the resulting solution is poured onto a surface covered with grease, the tails of the detergent molecules will dissolve in the grease. The polar heads of the molecules, however, not being soluble in grease, will remain within the aqueous part of the system (a). Put another way, the detergent molecules seem to stick into the grease layer as if they were a lot of tiny straight pins. If some agitation—stirring, boiling, or tumbling—is now added, the grease film will break up into small globules. But as the grease starts to break up, each tiny globule becomes "pincushioned" by detergent molecules (b). In this condition, the grease is in the form of a stable emulsion. That is, the grease remains suspended in the mixture. Each globule, its surface studded with the polar heads of the detergent molecules, is in effect a sphere whose surface is covered with a layer of similarly charged particles (c).

Now let's take a closer look at the probable structure of one of these emulsified globules. In Figure 8-4, the globule has been blown up

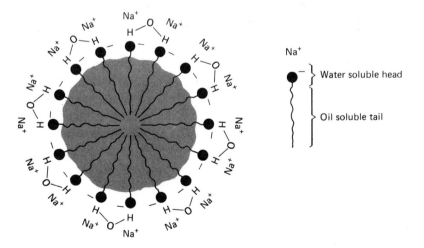

Figure 8-4. In a micelle, the oil soluble tails of detergent molecules are dissolved in the globule of oil or grease, while the water soluble heads are dissolved in the detergent solution.

enough in cross section to show the positions of the detergent molecules. If you imagine this two-dimensional drawing as a solid, you can picture the sphere of grease with many detergent-molecule tails all pointing toward the center of the sphere. Tiny droplets of oil or grease such as this one do not come together, or coagulate, to form a large globule because of the layer of negative charge on the outside of each globule. This charge is negative, of course, because each detergent molecule is a salt, and salts ionize in aqueous solution. Thus the negative ends of the detergent molecules attract polar water molecules, which in turn attract and hold the sodium (or potassium) ions that originally came from the detergent molecules. When a particle has adjacent to its surface a double layer of charges of opposite sign, the particle is called a *micelle*. Micelles tend to repel each other because the outer layers on adjacent particles all have the same electrical charge. Like charges repel each other, as you are well aware. In this emulsified, or suspended form, the grease globules are easily rinsed away.

So far, for the sake of simplicity, detergents have been referred to as if they are all sodium or potassium salts. But this need not be the case at all. Sodium- and potassium-containing detergent molecules are said to be *anionic* because the water soluble portion of the molecule carries a negative charge in solution. Anionic detergents are by far the most important. *Nonionic* detergent molecules also consist of the head and tail structure, but in their case the head group is generally the hydroxyl (—OH) group. In *cationic* molecules, the head group is a nitrogen atom, which frequently has a halogen atom attached to it.

Preparation of Detergents

As pointed out earlier, detergents are manufactured by a process quite different from that used to prepare soaps. Let's look at the reactions for the preparation of a typical anionic detergent—sodium lauryl sulfate. This substance is obtained from lauryl alcohol—$CH_3(CH_2)_{10}CH_2OH$—and sulfuric acid. Lauryl alcohol is the principal alcohol derived from the chemical breakdown of coconut oil. The alcohol and sulfuric acid react as follows:

$$CH_3(CH_2)_{10}CH_2\underline{OH} + \underline{H}OSO_2OH \longrightarrow H_2O + CH_3(CH_2)_{10}CH_2OSO_2OH$$

lauryl hydrogen sulfate

If this product is then treated with alkali (NaOH), the sodium salt of the hydrogen sulfate is formed. This is the detergent molecule.

$$CH_3(CH_2)_{10}CH_2OSO_2O\underline{H} + Na^+\underline{OH}^- \longrightarrow H_2O + CH_3(CH_2)_{10}CH_2OSO_2O^-Na^+$$

sodium lauryl sulfate

As this example suggests, the major raw material for detergent manufacture is some form of oil. Here the oil is coconut oil, a vegetable oil. For many other detergents the oil is refined from petroleum. These oils —called petroleum hydrocarbons—consist of long-chain molecules such as the 12-carbon chain $[CH_3(CH_2)_{10}CH_2—]$ of lauryl alcohol. These chains are both linear and branched and may even contain rings of carbon atoms.

For example, before the introduction of "soft," or biodegradable detergents in 1966, detergent molecules typically had molecular structures that included a benzene ring and branched-chain hydrocarbons. But as it turned out, detergent molecules containing branched-chain and cyclic hydrocarbons resist biological breakdown. Put another way, these structures are highly resistant to oxidation, even by microorganisms. In a manner of speaking, they are indigestible to the bacteria that normally decompose sewage. On the other hand, the same microorganisms readily decompose detergents containing straight-chain hydrocarbons.

Thus the task of producing "soft" detergents came down to a laboratory problem that was simple in theory, but somewhat more difficult in practice. All that was needed was to prune the side branches and carbon rings from the molecules. The molecule this would produce should be the ideal detergent. It should have excellent wetting ability and cleansing properties, but at the same time be nearly 100 percent biodegradable.

How this was accomplished is shown in the equations of Figure 8-5. The detergent molecule is sodium alkane sulfonate (SAS); it is 99 percent biodegradable. As you can see, the backbone of SAS is completely linear—there are no side groups along the carbon chain of the hydrocarbon portion of the molecule. In addition, the molecule contains no benzene or cyclic groups. The sulfonate groups ($—SO_3Na$) are distributed along the hydrocarbon chains, which average about 14 to 18 carbon atoms long. The process illustrated here starts with straight-chain hydrocarbons, which are first irradiated by gamma radiation in the presence of sulfur dioxide and oxygen. This produces the acid form of the detergent molecule—the hydrogen alkane sulfonate. In the final step—the same one employed by Fremy when he discovered the first crude detergent—this substance is treated with alkali. The result is the sodium alkane sulfonate molecule.

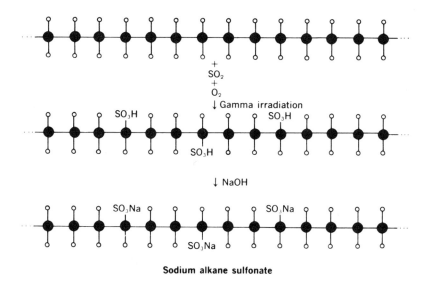

Sodium alkane sulfonate

Figure 8-5.   How 99 percent biodegradable sodium alkane sulfonate (SAS) was first produced.

But despite the fact that biodegradable molecules are now used in detergents, the threat of pollution has not been completely eliminated. On Long Island, for example, residents heaved a great sigh of relief when biodegradable detergents appeared on the market. It seemed as if their detergent pollution problem was at an end. In due time it was relieved, but strangely enough, clearing up the foam problem revealed another, more serious problem. As the foam began to disappear, Suffolk County health officials made the discouraging discovery that the detergent foam had been masking sewage. The great increase in population, accompanied by the installation of thousands of cesspools and septic tanks, had so overloaded the soil with pollutants that the naturally-occurring bacteria couldn't possibly keep up. Today no detergents may be sold in Suffolk County; the pollution problem, however, remains.

Phosphates and Eutrophication

As this is being written, yet another pollution problem related to detergents has entered the limelight. This is the use of phosphates mixed with the detergent to increase cleaning power. A recent Department of the Interior study revealed that the percentage of phosphates in detergents in use in the United States ranges from a low of 14 percent to a high of 74 percent. The Government has urged manufacturers to reduce or eliminate the phosphate content. By the time you read this, laws forbidding the use of phosphates in detergents may be in effect in many states. There's a good possibility, however, that such laws may not be in force throughout the United States. Thus, you should understand the nature of the phosphate problem.

Is there a clear, unpolluted stream, pond, or lake in your area? Or has the water, crystal clear just a few years ago, turned cloudy, or perhaps even the color of pea soup? If you answer a remorseful "yes" to the second question, phosphates from detergents may be part of the problem.

Phosphates, as you know, contain phosphorus, an element essential for plant growth. Thus, the phosphates in detergents are in effect a plant nutrient. Now, when laundry water is discarded, it is eventually returned to the soil as groundwater. The bulk of the phosphate returns to the soil with the water because it is not biodegradable by the organisms that attack and decompose detergents and sewage. Thus, when this waste water runs into streams, lakes, and ponds, the phosphates are carried with it.

At this point you have probably anticipated the rest of the story. Algae and other plant life feed on the phosphates, and multiply in vast numbers. But these plants, now choking the water, eventually die and decay. The decay process that follows then uses up the available oxygen in the water, thereby causing the death of all forms of aquatic life. The result is a stinking, decaying organic soup. The process is called *eutrophication;* it is a growing problem in many of our lakes and rivers.

Recognizing this problem, Canada and Sweden have both taken action. Canada, for example, has placed a total ban on phosphates in detergents, the ban to be effective by 1972. The United States, on the other hand, has adopted a more moderate tone. At first, when the role of phosphates in the process of eutrophication was widely publicized, an intensive search for effective substitutes was started. New products without phosphates appeared and promised the same cleansing ability as those with phosphates. But the new additives being used in place of phosphates were soon revealed to be dangerous to people, and therefore highly undesirable. The outcome of this dilemma? A compromise. The U.S. Government now recommends the use of phosphates as the least of several evils. And our precious bodies of fresh water continue, with the help of the nation's housewives and others, along the eutrophication route to useless swamps.

Detergents, plus the additives used to improve their efficiency, clearly exhibit some of the properties of a double-edged sword. We may be the cleanest nation in the world, but we may have sacrificed much of our natural environment while achieving this dubious distinction.

9

THE "DIRTY SEVEN"—Molecular Miracle Turned Monster

During the 1940s, Nobel Prizes were awarded to the discoverers of nuclear fission and the pesticidal properties of DDT. Both DDT and the first atom bomb were used during World War II. Both receive credit for saving countless lives. The atom bombings of Hiroshima and Nagasaki are said to have prevented the loss of hundreds of thousands of additional lives by effectively halting the war in the Pacific. DDT's effectiveness is revealed in the statement that World War II was the first war in history during which more soldiers died from battle wounds than from typhus, a louse-borne disease. Today these claims seem to have a hollow ring, for both nuclear energy and chlorinated hydrocarbon pesticides have invaded the civilian world and endanger the welfare of people everywhere. Indeed, taken together they now pose the most serious threat ever to the earth's environment. This threat is *fallout.* In much the same manner that radioactive fallout from bomb tests spreads and contaminates, DDT and its chemical relatives threaten the entire world.

Nuclear bomb tests in the atmosphere (with the exception of Chinese tests) have been halted, and man is hopeful that he has brought under control the danger from radioactive fallout. This is not the case with chlorinated hydrocarbon pesticides. Astonishing as it may seem, some of the DDT sprayed during the mid 1940s is still in the environment here in the early 1970s. It is this persistence that makes these chemicals a greater potential threat than radioactive fallout. Moreover, less is known about how long the pesticides will last, or of their physiological effects.

A Problem for Your Children's Children

The term *environmental half-life* is used to express the persistence of a chemical in the environment. This is the time required for one-half of the chemical in the environment to disappear—usually through chemical breakdown. The environmental half-life of DDT is not accurately known, but estimates range between 10 and 20 years. When you consider that as you read these words, almost two pounds of DDT have been dispersed for each acre of the world's arable land, the magnitude of the long-range problem becomes clear. It has been estimated that about one billion pounds of DDT are today circulating in the environment. Chlorinated hydrocarbon pesticide residues will probably be a problem for as long as you live. Your children, and then theirs, will have to cope with other problems generated by these residues.

As with many other major scientific discoveries, the saga of chlorinated hydrocarbon pesticides started with a seemingly insignificant event. A German scientist, working on his doctoral thesis in 1874, synthesized the compound dichloro-diphenyl-trichloroethane. This, of course, is DDT. Some 60 years then passed before the compound was studied for its properties as an insecticide. Just before World War II, its toxicity to insects was established with tests on wine grape pests and American striped potato beetles that had spread to Europe. Then, during that war, DDT came into its own. The first massive application came in Naples, Italy, just after the city was liberated. A widespread epidemic of typhus had broken out; allied troops as well as the native population were in great danger. The epidemic was halted dramatically in just a few days by measures that would horrify observers today. First, people were dusted with a mixture that contained DDT, and second, the insecticide was sprayed heavily throughout the area. As World War II progressed DDT was used extensively, especially in areas where insect infestation was heavy. In the South Pacific, for example, it was sprayed widely from airplanes to control malaria.

The "Dirty Seven"

DDT was the first of the chlorinated hydrocarbon insecticides. Its startling and dramatic toxicity to insects, of course, immediately spurred intensive research into other possible insecticides with a similar chemical composition. The result is a group of compounds that came to be known as the "dirty seven" during the late 1960s. These are dieldrin, heptachlor, aldrin, benzene hexachloride, endrin, chlordane, and DDT. The structural formulas of these compounds, including the two common forms of DDT, are shown in Figure 9-1.

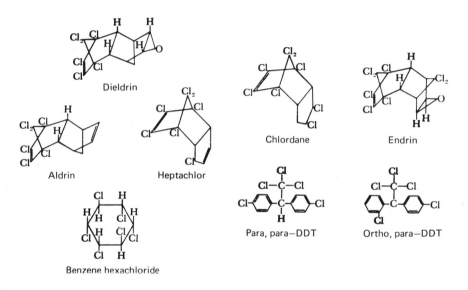

Figure 9-1. The structural formulas of the "dirty seven." Today several pesticides other than these also threaten wildlife and the environment.

Every one of these substances poses the same threat to the environment. They are all practically insoluble in water, resist decomposition in the environment, and have a broad spectrum effect—that is, they kill indiscriminately, both pest and nonpest insects. While most of what follows is based on findings about DDT, keep in mind that it applies also to the remainder of the dirty seven.

The case against DDT began to be taken seriously when the pesticide was found in birds, fish, and seals in Antarctica, thousands of miles from the nearest place of use. In addition, DDT has been found in polar bear tissue in the Arctic. Now it is generally conceded that the compound pollutes our entire environment. It is present in rain and surface water in parts per trillion, but people carry it about in their fatty tissues in concentrations a million times greater—between 5 and 20 parts per million (ppm). Even human milk contains DDT. Thus, it is passed along to infants by nursing mothers.

How does DDT spread in the environment? To begin with, there is a great deal of it. Thus, it is spread by just about every mechanism available. Run-off water picks up some from forests and agricultural lands, and then drains into rivers, streams, and ponds. Some finds its way into groundwater by passing unchanged through sewage treatment plants. Contamination of freshwater bodies constitutes a very serious problem because of the phenomenon of *biological magnification.* For example, as this is written DDT is present in the bottom sediments of Lake Michigan at a concentration of about 0.0085 ppm. Tiny invertebrate organisms that feed on the bottom sediments, however, contain DDT in concentrations about 50 times higher—0.43 ppm. But fish feed on these tiny organisms and concentrate the DDT even further. The fish carry from 3 to 8 ppm in their tissues. Gulls and other birds that prey on live fish then complete the chain by concentrating the insecticide to levels as high as 3000 ppm.

DDT's major dispersal route appears to be atmospheric. As the insecticide is sprayed, only about one-half reaches its destination. The other half drifts away to settle somewhere else, or it is carried into the upper atmosphere only to reach the earth again in rainfall. For example, over 40 tons of DDT and its relatives are deposited on England each year by rainfall. The DDT that does reach the ground is redistributed by two additional means. In one, it evaporates with water and is carried back into the atmosphere. In the other, it is carried along as wind blows about fine particles of agricultural soil. In one instance, a dust storm originating in Texas produced a DDT fallout in Ohio. The DDT in the dust particles ranged from 3 to 80 ppm.

At this point you're probably wondering if DDT undergoes any chemical breakdown at all in the environment. The answer is "yes," some decomposition does take place. Partial breakdown through such processes as enzymatic action and ultraviolet radiation results in the removal of one chlorine atom, and yields the compound DDE. Unfortunately, DDE is also toxic, but probably less so than DDT. DDE also is found widely in the environment, and has been implicated in some of the toxic effects that are described below. DDE, for example, inhibits photosynthesis in marine phytoplankton (microscopic plants) to an extent three times greater than that of DDT. We need only mention that marine phytoplankton supply about 70 percent of the world's oxygen through photosynthesis to bring home the gravity of the problem.

Long-Term Consequences

What are the long-term consequences on the environment of DDT and its chemical sisters? Some of the answers to this question are known. Unfortunately, however, what we now know seems to be roughly analogous to the part of an iceberg that appears above the surface of the water. Much, much more is hidden and yet to be learned. If this is true, then the outlook is bleak indeed, for what we do know spells great danger for many species as well as for the quality of the natural environment. Let's look at some of these consequences, keeping in mind that these effects may very well represent just the beginning.

The indiscriminate application of chlorinated hydrocarbon pesticides effectively reduces a variety of wildlife in an area. This occurs because the pesticides virtually eliminate sensitive species, thus allowing the less sensitive organisms to increase in their place. The result is that we have fewer dragonflies and more mosquitoes, fewer insectivorous birds and more grackles and starlings, fewer trout and more coarse fish.

Shortly after DDT began to be used in civilian life, the problem of *resistance* appeared. As early as 1946, certain populations of houseflies were reported to be resistant to DDT. By 1948 the number of species of insects resistant to the pesticide had jumped to 12. By 1957 the list included 76 species. Today some 224 pest insects are resistant to one or more of the chlorinated hydrocarbon pesticides. Ninety-seven of these insect pests are a public health or veterinary concern, and 127 are insects that attack stored goods, field crops, or valuable forest species.

Resistance to pesticides is a classic example of selection. Application of the pesticide kills off the members of a species most susceptible, leaving behind only those that are somehow tolerant of the poison. These organisms then breed and a population emerges that is unaffected by the pesticide. In one instance, the salt-marsh sandfly became resistant to dieldrin after only three applications of just one pound of dieldrin per acre of marsh. What is even more important, the resistant insects were also resistant to several other pesticides.

A secondary problem related to the use of chlorinated hydrocarbon pesticides, that is, *resurgence* of pest populations, has also been described. In this case the problem arises when pesticides that are more toxic but less persistent are substituted for the chlorinated hydrocarbon pesticides. In most instances the substituted pesticide has been an organophosphate. Such compounds have very great toxicity; when applied they literally wipe out all insects, including many of the natural insect enemies of pest insects. But organophosphates break down quite rapidly. Thus, as soon as they have decomposed and lost their toxicity, pests from neighboring fields move in and build up very rapidly, with no natural enemies to block their rapid population growth. This is resurgence. The only answer to this problem is a bad answer; increased frequency of pesticide application and increased concentrations. Hardly the ultimate answer to the insect pest problem.

Another significant problem is the phenomenon of pest *trade-off.* All agricultural ecosystems contain numerous insects whose populations remain small because of the presence of a variety of natural enemies. When pesticides are introduced into the ecosystem, however, this delicate balance may be upset. The result is that nonpests may become pests, and increase the difficulty of establishing control. Trade-offs have occurred often; today, as a result, the list of insect pests is increasing, not decreasing, as one might expect from the widespread use of powerful insecticides.

A good example of trade-off is the appearance of bollworms and spider mites in the cotton-growing area of Louisiana. For many generations, insect control in the cotton country was aimed at the boll weevil. Chlorinated hydrocarbon pesticides such as DDT were used widely. But then in 1955 it was discovered that the boll weevil had developed resistance to these compounds, and it was necessary to switch to organophosphates. The drastic effect of this switch first led to resurgence and, of course, since their natural enemies had been wiped out, the bollworm and spider mite were free to reproduce to the point where they became major pests. This is not an isolated instance. Moreover, in other areas of the country these new pests have gotten completely out of control. In Texas and California, for example, spider mites and bollworms have developed resistance to all pesticides. As this is being written, no currently available insecticide will control these insects.

The list continues, and we now come to *acute toxicity.* Many species of wildlife are susceptible to DDT and similar compounds. For example, it has been reported that robins feeding on insects and worms around DDT-treated elm trees have ingested enough DDT to cause death. In many instances, toxic doses of the pesticide have been stored in the fatty tissue of an organism; no harm comes to the animal as long as its normal food supply is maintained. Should the animal be deprived of food, however, as in migration or starvation, metabolism of the stored fat will release the pesticide into the bloodstream. Often the quantity released is enough to kill the animal. This is known to have occurred in robins.

Rather low concentrations of DDT can result in the acute poisoning and death of many species of fish. In other fish, particularly marine species, another form of poisoning may occur—chronic toxicity in the young. This phenomenon has been studied in lake trout. In these fish, the relatively low levels of 0.5 to 2.9 ppm of DDT have little or no effect on adult fish, although freshly hatched fish larvae may be killed. DDT concentrates in fatty tissue. Thus, when eggs are formed in the female fish, the yolk of the eggs picks up some DDT. After fertilization, the growing embryo obtains all of its nourishment from the yolk prior to hatching. But as the yolk is used up, the concentration of DDT becomes higher and higher. Finally, as the last of the yolk is absorbed, the highly concentrated DDT is released into the body of the larva. If the level of DDT is too high, death results. There is evidence also to suggest that even if the young fish survives, adverse changes in its behavioral patterns will occur. Such changes could greatly affect the fish's ability to cope with its environment.

Table 9-1 gives DDT concentrations for numerous freshwater, coastal, and oceanic organisms. These concentrations, recorded between 1966 and 1969, are undoubtedly low compared to today's. For example, the concentration given for Coho salmon in Lake Michigan is 10 ppm. During 1969, however, a 28,000-pound shipment of Coho was seized and destroyed because the fish contained an average of 19 ppm. The Coho salmon, introduced into the Greak Lakes to control the alewife population, took to its task immediately. Within just a few years it became a major game fish. Today the Coho is fun to catch, but few people want to risk putting it on the dining room table.

Both acute and chronic toxicity have been reported in birds. In addition to the deaths of robins mentioned previously, other birds have been found dead or dying as a result of DDT poisoning. For example, during the spring of 1969 large numbers of cormorants and murres were found dead or dying on California beaches. The dying birds had nervous tremors similar to those connected with DDT poisoning. In addition, the birds were all in an advanced state of emaciation. Analysis of tissues taken from these birds revealed extremely high concentrations of DDT in the liver and other organs. It seems quite probable that the birds, experiencing difficulty finding adequate food, had turned to the metabolism of fatty tissue for energy. But this apparently released stored DDT into the bloodstream, and death resulted.

Chronic DDT toxicity in birds poses an even greater threat. In this case, DDT in the tissues of adult female birds causes the formation of thin eggshells. The exact mechanism for this effect is unknown, although several possibilities have been suggested. In one, it is suggested that DDT interferes with the metabolism of the female hormone, estrogen. Another possibility is interference with thyroid hormone metabolism. And finally, inhibition of the enzyme, carbonic anhydrase, has

TABLE 9-1: DDT IN FRESHWATER AND MARINE ORGANISMS

Species	DDT (ppm)
Freshwater fishes (flesh)	
Largemouth bass (Calif.)	1.97
Channel catfish (Calif.)	4.02
White catfish (Calif.)	1.01
Yellow perch (Calif.)	0.07
Rainbow trout	0.17
Coho salmon (Lake Michigan)	10.00
Atlantic coast estuary treated with DDT for mosquito control (DDT values for whole organism)	
Zooplankton	0.04
Shrimp	0.16
Mud-snail	0.26
3-spine stickleback	0.26
Sheepshead minnow	0.94
Summer flounder	1.28
Atlantic needlefish	2.07
Common tern	3.15−5.17
Herring gull	3.52−18.5
Least tern	4.75−6.40
Pacific Ocean, coastal (levels for whole animal unless stated otherwise)	
Common mussel	0.019−0.120
Common starfish	0.020
Squid	0.028
Short-spired purple snail	0.094−0.163
Sand crab	0.080−0.220
Rock crab	0.491−0.500
Northern anchovy: San Francisco	0.59
Monterey	0.90
Morro Bay	3.04
Los Angeles	14.00
English sole: San Francisco	0.55
Monterey	0.76
Shiner perch (San Francisco)	1.17
Jack mackerel (Santa Barbara)	0.56
Bluefin tuna (Baja California)	0.56
Western gull	9.20
Western gull (liver), dead bird	800.00
Cassin's auklet	1.0−15.4
Brandt's cormorant	4.4
Brown pelican (breast muscle)	84.4
Pacific Ocean, open seas − Birds	
Red phalarope	1.0
Fulmar	1.9
Sooty shearwater	8.4
Slender-billed shearwater	32.00

been suggested. This enzyme plays a role in the deposition of calcium carbonate in the eggshell.

Whatever the cause, however, the end result is the same. Females lay eggs with shells so thin they break under the pressure of the mother's sitting on them. Already this effect has severely limited the reproductive capability of many birds, especially those high in the food chain. Birds of prey and those that feed on fish, such as the peregrine falcon, bald eagle, osprey, and brown pelican have all been hit very hard. On the East Coast, for example, several major osprey nesting regions are now almost totally unpopulated during the mating season. Another tragic case is the failure of the pelicans on Anacapa Island, off Santa Barbara, California. In a survey of 300 nests made during the spring of 1969, only 12 intact eggs were found. Of these, only three hatched. The majority of the pelicans were either sitting on crushed eggs, or they had given up nesting completely.

Needed—Safer Insect Controls

Proponents of continued use of DDT may argue that the loss of a few species of fish and birds is more than compensated for by savings in human life. For the short term this may be the case, although safer methods of insect control are now available. For the long view, however, another point of view is needed. Widespread destruction of species of wildlife is today a symptom—a symptom of worldwide disruption of ecological checks and balances. What the ultimate effect on the environment will be, no one can predict. We know enough, however, to recognize that man is a part of the environment, and that any major disruption of ecological balances *must* inevitably have an adverse effect on man's well-being as a species.

But what of adverse physiological effects on man himself? There is certainly room for apprehension, although no direct evidence for any such effects has yet been uncovered. Why the concern, if no evidence has been uncovered? To begin with, we know of course that DDT and its relatives are highly toxic, and that they are stored in the fatty tissues of man as well as that of other species. The table that follows gives the quantities found in human fat taken from a number of different geographic regions.

DDT IN HUMAN FAT SAMPLES

Regions	ppm	Region	ppm
Arctic regions	3	France	5.2
Canada	4.9	Hungary	12.4
U.S.A.	12	India (New	
Germany	2.3	Delhi)	26
England	3.9	Israel	19.2

DDT has been found in the human brain also. In a recent study, autopsies were done on persons showing a history of neurological, brain, or liver disorders. The results of these autopsies were then compared to controls. In all cases the DDT levels in brain, liver, and fat were higher than in the tissues of the controls. Whether these higher concentrations were significant in the cause of the diseases, however, is unknown.

Determining the precise physiological effects on man of a substance such as DDT is very difficult. Obviously, it is impossible to experiment directly with human subjects. This leaves the results of experiments with laboratory animals. Extrapolation of such results to man is a tricky and imprecise art, but it is the only technique available. In such studies, if a chemical produces adverse effects on two or more mammals such as rats, mice, or rabbits, it is assumed that the chemical will probably have similar adverse effects on man. On the other hand, if the chemical has no effect on two or more mammals, then it is assumed that man will be unaffected. Large doses of the chemical being studied are often given to small numbers of animals. The results are then used to infer the effects of small doses absorbed by large numbers of people. This procedure, indirect and highly imprecise, is the best available at the present time. It is standard procedure in the science of toxicology.

Another type of conjecture is direct comparison between man and species affected by DDT. For example, mammals and birds have similar sex hormones, and similar mechanisms for controlling metabolism.

Environmental levels of DDT, as you recall, affect reproduction in birds. Who is to say that these effects might not strike man as well if the environmental levels should become sufficiently high? Even more ominous, a low level chronic toxicity and adverse effects on reproduction in man may already be taking place.

Although the story is far from complete, other effects have been described. To date only DDT has been studied in any depth for its effects on mammals. We know now that it permanently damages the nervous system, and that it impairs nervous functions in a number of ways. It also damages the liver, affects the function of the thyroid gland, and interferes with the activity of certain enzymes. Its presence in the body changes the effects of certain drugs and poisons, and stimulates the breakdown of natural sex hormones. In some instances it has the same effect as the female sex hormone estrogen, and reduces fertility. For example, when young roosters are exposed to DDT, they mature with smaller-than-normal testicles.

A number of chlorinated hydrocarbon pesticides have been identified as *carcinogens,* that is, agents that cause cancer. Included are DDT, aldrin, dieldrin, heptachlor, and DDD. *Mutagenesis*—changes in the genetic material—may also be caused by certain pesticides. Dieldrin is known to be a mutagen, and others are under suspicion. A problem here is that many commonly-used pesticides have not been tested adequately. We know very little about their potential danger to man as well as to wildlife.

What of the Future?

What does this unhappy story tell us for the future? Should we turn back all chemical pesticides, and run the risk of being overwhelmed by insect pests? Or is there a middle ground? DDT seems to be the focal point of this controversy. Its use in U.S. agriculture is to be eliminated by 1972, although no change is expected overseas. No one can predict just when the remainder of the world community will recognize the threat, and ban its use.

In the meantime, research may produce better pesticides. A good pesticide must be nonpersistent in the environment, and nonmobile—it must stay where it is applied. Such a pesticide must also break down rapidly in the environment, and be more selective in its toxicity. In addition, it must be incapable of being concentrated by living matter. A tall order, this perfect pesticide, and relatively unlikely, too.

Biological control of pests—the most logical but perhaps the most difficult solution—has been elevated in importance since the hue and cry about DDT. Harmless insects that prey on pests are particularly important. These natural enemies of insect pests do exist. Unfortunately, agricultural measures taken to eliminate the pests also eliminate the beneficial insects. What is now needed, and in fact is already in use in many areas, is a balanced blending of chemical and biological insect control techniques.

Figure 9-2.   One example of biological control. In this photo an aphid lion is attacking a cotton bollworm, a serious agricultural pest. The aphid lion, larva of the green lacewing, feeds on the bollworm's body fluids. Artificial insect eggs are used to raise aphid lions in numbers large enough to be effective as a control. (Photo courtesy of Southwest Research Institute)

The experience of the cotton industry of Peru illustrates how bad things can become, and how intelligent management of pests can reverse the situation and yield satisfactory crops. In 1943 Peruvian cotton growers in the Cañete Valley were harvesting some 406 pounds of cotton per acre. Chlorinated hydrocarbon pesticides were then introduced widely in 1949. By 1954 yields had increased to a record average of 649 pounds per acre. At this point the trouble began. The number of pest species jumped from seven to thirteen, and several developed resistance to the pesticides in use. Yields began to drop off sharply, and by 1956 had fallen to an average of 296 pounds per acre. During some of the worst growing seasons, 15 to 25 applications of pesticides, both alone and in mixtures, failed to control harmful insects because of resistance.

In response to this drastic situation, an entirely new pest control program was devised. Less emphasis was placed on synthetic poisons, and more was placed on biological controls. This balanced attack began to produce positive results immediately, and by 1960 the Cañete Valley produced a record average of 923 pounds per acre.

In the past, the only price of using chlorinated hydrocarbon pesticides seemed to be the low cost of the chemicals themselves. Now we know better. Today the effectiveness of the chemicals in terms of crop and health protection has reached an all-time low, while their cost in terms of dollars and disruption of the environment is rising rapidly. Clearly, man must begin to utilize control methods that give the desired crop yields, but at the same time pose no threat to the environment. The stakes are high indeed, for the ultimate fate of the planet itself depends upon what choice man makes.

10

POLYMERS—Giant Molecules Come of Age

When historians look back at the mid-twentieth century, they will be tempted to call it either the "atomic age" or the "space age." They could be wrong on both counts. It's possible that the shock and excitement potential of nuclear power and the moon landings will overshadow a more pervasive yet less dramatic development—the rise of polymer science. The "polymer age." Try it on for size. Sounds odd, doesn't it? And yet, with close examination polymers appear to have had a far greater effect on the everyday life of mid-twentieth century man than either nuclear power or the space program. Think about it for a moment. Polymer products have invaded virtually every area of our lives. From Dacron neckties, Orlon sweaters, and nylon stockings to polypropylene rope, silicone caulking compounds, and Teflon coatings inside pots and pans, we are literally surrounded by products manufactured from polymer molecules. Be it business, medicine, entertainment, recreation, or what have you, one or more polymer products are sure to be making your activities easier or more pleasant.

It was not always this way. Just a few years ago—some 30 to 40 to be more exact—chemists were avoiding polymer science. They did not understand the chemistry of high molecular weight compounds because the properties of these substances differed so greatly from the properties of small-molecule compounds. Indefinite molecular weights, indefinite melting points, and unpredictable chemical behavior all added up to a puzzle that seemed totally indecipherable.

Today, of course, just the opposite is true. Chemists not only know the chemical and physical properties of a large number of polymers,

Figure 10-1. "Space age" or "polymer age"? Man has conquered the moon, but could he have done it without polymers? For example, when Apollo 11's Neil Armstrong and Edwin Aldrin first stepped on the surface of the moon their boot soles were made of silicone rubber, a polymer characterized by high resistance to heat. (Photo courtesy of GE Silicone Products Department)

today they can engineer a polymer to fit a specified use—much as the custom tailor designs a suit to fit a particular man.

Polymer chemistry made its first great stride forward when it was discovered that polymers are held together by ordinary covalent bonds, and not by some sort of mysterious and elusive physical force. From this point on, the growth of polymer science has been rapid indeed, both in the synthesis of new compounds and in the study of naturally occurring polymers. Surprising as it may seem, the molecules most important to life are polymers. Cellulose, the chief component of plant cell walls; proteins, essential compounds in all living cells; nucleic acids (e.g., DNA, RNA), substances essential for transmitting hereditary characteristics; all are polymers.

Polymer Structure

Polymer molecules, sometimes called "macromolecules," have very high molecular weights indeed, as the following table shows. This table compares simple molecules with polymer macromolecules. Note how the molecular weights jump. From water at 18 we jump to rubber at about 1,360,000. If we took this molecular weight in grams, we would have a cube of rubber weighing more than a ton and measuring more than a yard on each side!

MOLECULES AND MACROMOLECULES

Substance	Formula	Molecular Weight
Water	H_2O	18
Sugar	$C_{12}H_{22}O_{11}$	282
Cellulose	$(C_6H_{10}O_5)_{2,000}$	324,000
Rubber	$(C_5H_8)_{20,000}$	1,360,000

There is an essential simplicity to the molecular structure of polymers. This structure consists of giant molecules in long chains; the long chains are formed by the chemical union of a large number of low-molecular weight units called *monomers.* Added up, the molecular weights may range up into the millions, although most polymers of practical importance have molecular weights from a few thousand to a few hundred thousand. Table 10-1 shows the monomer molecule and the repeating structural unit for a number of well-known polymers. Just for the fun of it, can you name two or more commonly used items made from each of the polymers listed?

Table 10-1. — Some Well-Known Polymers

Polymer	Monomer(s)	Repeating Structural Unit
Polyethylene	$CH_2 = CH_2$	$- CH_2 - CH_2 -$
Polystyrene	$CH_2 = CH$ (phenyl)	$- CH_2 - CH -$ (phenyl)
Teflon	$CF_2 = CF_2$	$- CF_2 - CF_2 -$
Orlon	$CH_2 = CH$ CN	$- CH_2 - CH -$ CN
Dacron	$HOOC \bigcirc COOH$ $+$ $HOCH_2CH_2OH$	$- C \bigcirc C - OCH_2CH_2O -$ $\parallel \quad \parallel$ $O \quad\quad O$
Nylon	$H_2N(CH_2)_6NH_2$ $+$ $HOCO(CH_2)_4COOH$	$\quad\quad O \quad\quad O$ $\quad\quad \parallel \quad\quad \parallel$ $- NH(CH_2)_6C(CH_2)_4C -$

Knowledge of the chain structure of polymers yields a simple and useful way to classify the different structural possibilities. Thus, chemists speak of *linear, branched,* and *cross-linked* polymers. In order to represent these structures schematically, let's designate a letter, say X, to represent the repeating structural unit of the polymer. Remember that this repeating unit is derived from the monomer molecule. Using this notation, the linear type polymer is represented as

$$\ldots -X-X-X-X-X-X-X-X- \ldots$$

Teflon is a linear polymer; Table 10-1 shows the repeating molecular unit and the monomer.

Sometimes more than one monomeric unit combines at random, or regularly, in a polymer. Such substances are called *copolymers*. A linear copolymer with the functional units X and Y combined at random might have the following structure in an isolated segment:

$$\ldots -X-Y-XX-Y-X-YYY-XXX-Y- \ldots$$

If, on the other hand, the X and Y units repeat with perfect regularity, the substance is a polymer with the repeating functional group XY.

$$\ldots -XY-XY-XY-XY-XY- \ldots$$

Natural rubber is an example of a polymer that occurs in nature. Natural rubber occurs as a milky white emulsion of latex in water. It takes a considerable amount of physical and chemical treatment to turn out the product we are familiar with. But, chemical treatment and additives aside, the basic chemistry is simple.

Quantitative analysis tells us that rubber is a hydrocarbon with the empirical formula, $(C_5H_8)_n$. It is a high polymer, the monomer being isoprene, C_5H_8. The average molecular weight of natural rubber is over one million, as pointed out earlier.

The actual mechanism of chain formation in natural rubber is not as yet completely understood. Experimental evidence, however, shows that it consists of isoprene molecules joined head-to-tail. The chemist would call this multiple 1,4-addition.

Note that the polymerization reaction, shown in the equation that follows, results from the disappearance of one double bond in each isoprene molecule, followed by head-to-tail bonding.

$$CH_2{=}\overset{\overset{\displaystyle CH_3}{|}}{C}{-}CH{=}CH_2 + CH_2{=}\overset{\overset{\displaystyle CH_3}{|}}{C}{-}CH{=}CH_2 + CH_2{=}\overset{\overset{\displaystyle CH_3}{|}}{C}{-}CH{=}CH_2$$

Isoprene

$$\downarrow$$

$$\cdots CH_2{-}\overset{\overset{\displaystyle CH_3}{|}}{C}{=}CH{-}CH_2{-}CH_2{-}\overset{\overset{\displaystyle CH_3}{|}}{C}{=}CH{-}CH_2{-}CH_2{-}\overset{\overset{\displaystyle CH_3}{|}}{C}{=}CH{-}CH_2 \cdots$$

Rubber

Thus, rubber contains one double bond per isoprene unit, located at the 2,3-position in each C_5 section. In addition, x-ray diffraction studies have shown that stretched rubber has a regular, ordered structure. As the following schematic diagram shows, the polymer molecule is such that the same attached units are on the same side of the double bond. This is the *cis* configuration.

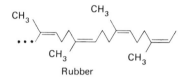

Rubber

If the attached groups are on opposite sides of the double bond, the structure is said to be *trans*. Styrene-butadiene synthetic rubber is an example of a random copolymer. This rubber is used for all passenger car tires manufactured in the United States. The monomers are styrene, $CH_2CHC_6H_5$, and butadiene, $CH_2CHCHCH_2$. Roughly three parts of butadiene and one part of styrene by weight combine to produce a polymer that contains six butadiene molecular units to every one styrene molecular unit. Both nylon and Dacron are examples of copolymers with a regularly repeating unit made up of two monomer molecules. These units are shown in Table 10-1.

Branching and Cross-Linking

To form a linear polymer the monomer units must have *two* reactive sites. For example, to form the linear polymer polyethylene, the double bond in ethylene, $(H_2C{=}CH_2)$ breaks producing a reactive site at each end of the molecule: $—CH_2—CH_2—$. These then join together to form polyethylene, $[—CH_2—CH_2—]_n$. Suppose, however, that monomer molecules with more than two reactive sites exist. Clearly, with this type of molecule available branched and cross-linked polymers become possible. If X represents a monomer molecule with two reactive sites, and A a monomer molecule with three reactive sites, then a branched polymer might appear as follows:

```
...—X—X—A—X—X—A—X—X—A—X—...
       |         |         |
       X         X         X
       |         |         |
       X         X         X
       |         |         |
       X         X         •
       |         |         •
       X         •         •
       |         •
       •         •
       •
       •
```

Cross-linked structures result when branched-chain polymer molecules interconnect. Cross-linked networks are usually very irregular, because polymerization is a random process. A possible cross-linked structure is shown here:

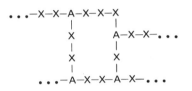

A simple example will show how both branching and cross-linking may occur. When polyethylene is irradiated, reactions such as the following occur. In this case the energy of the incident radiation removes a pair of hydrogen atoms, and a carbon-to-carbon bond forms. A cross-link is shown here. Branching is also possible.

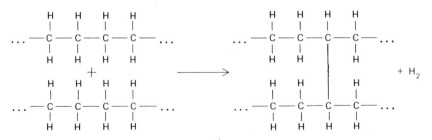

Do you like to play with models? A good way to picture polymer molecules is by paper clip models. Fasten the clips end to end to form chains. Wrap each clip with colored tape to identify the number of reactive sites on the "molecule." How could you construct models of branched and cross-linked molecules?

Reaction Mechanisms

A useful chemical classification of polymers is based on the reaction mechanism by which the polymer was formed. In this scheme two broad classes are identified—*condensation* polymers and *addition* polymers.

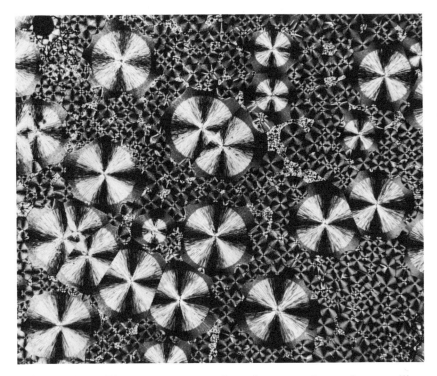

Figure 10-2. The gross structure of a polymer can be partly crystalline and partly amorphous. In this polarized light micrograph, the circular areas are crystalline; the other parts show amorphous domains. (Photo courtesy of GE Research and Development Center)

In condensation reactions, two molecules react to form a new molecule, but a small group of atoms is lost during the reaction. Thus, the new molecule is slightly smaller than the sum of the original two molecules. For example, an organic acid and an alcohol react to produce an ester, with one molecule of water being eliminated during the reaction.

$$CH_3 COOH + C_2 H_5 OH \longrightarrow CH_3 COOC_2 H_5 + H_2 O$$

Suppose, however, that the molecules entering into the reaction each have two reactive sites, rather than one as in the instance above. As an example, consider the reaction between ethylene glycol ($HOCH_2CH_2OH$) and terephthalic acid ($HOOCC_6H_4COOH$). The reaction goes as follows, with two molecules of water being eliminated during formation of each of the repeating molecular units:

$$HOCH_2 CH_2 OH$$
$$+ \qquad \xrightarrow{-2H_2 O} \ldots -OCC_6 H_4 COOCH_2 CH_2 O- \ldots$$
$$HOOCC_6 H_4 COOH$$

This compound is of course Dacron, although it doesn't look much like a tie or dress here.

The second broad class of polymerization reaction mechanisms is addition reactions. The basic mechanism of addition polymerization starts with the activation of the monomer molecule. If X is the monomer molecule, this reaction is shown as:

$$X \longrightarrow X^*$$

This activated molecule can then attack and add to hundreds or even thousands of additional monomer molecules. The result is the rapid growth of an individual polymer chain:

$$X^* + X \longrightarrow X_2^* \xrightarrow{X} X_3^* \xrightarrow{X} X_4^* \longrightarrow \ldots X_n^*$$

The polymerization reaction terminates when the activated molecule loses its activation energy:

$$X_n{}^* \longrightarrow X_n$$

The formation of Teflon, now familiar as the coating on "greaseless" frying pans and other cookware, as well as on saw blades, snow shovels, and other tools, is an addition polymerization reaction. This polymerization begins with tetrafluoroethylene ($CF_2{=}CF_2$), an unsaturated molecule with two reactive sites. When this substance is catalyzed with oxygen, the polymerization reaction produces the linear polymer chain:

$$nCF_2 = CF_2 \longrightarrow (-CF_2-CF_2-)_n$$

Teflon

In unsaturated monomers such as tetrafluoroethylene ($CF_2{=}CF_2$) and ethylene itself ($CH_2{=}CH_2$), the mechanism of polymerization depends upon how the double bond is attacked. This in turn is usually controlled by the type of "catalyst" or activator used. And finally, the types of available "catalysts" or activators are classified in terms of the active species they are capable of generating. Three such possibilities exist: *free radicals, cations,* and *anions.*

In free radical polymerization, the free radical must first be generated. Free radicals are atoms or molecular fragments having a free unpaired electron. Such particles are, of course, highly reactive. Many organic and inorganic compounds yield free radicals when they are decomposed by heat or high-frequency radiation. For example, the compound benzoyl peroxide decomposes when heated to form two different free radicals. In these equations, a single dot is used to represent the unpaired electron.

$$(C_6H_5COO)_2 \longrightarrow 2C_6H_5COO\cdot$$

$$2C_6H_5COO\cdot \longrightarrow 2C_6H_5\cdot + 2CO_2$$

Radicals thus formed react with monomers, that is, they attack the double bond of the monomer, as follows. If we let $R\cdot$ represent the free radical, a typical reaction would be:

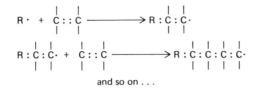

and so on . . .

In cationic polymerization, the double bond of the monomer is attacked by a cation—an atom or molecular group lacking a pair of electrons. Cations are, of course, positively charged. They are therefore strong electron acceptors. It follows that cations will react readily with double-bonded monomers that are strong electron donors. Numerous compounds, including $AlCl_3$, $AlBr_3$, BF_3, and $SnCl_4$, are suitable for use as catalysts in this type of polymerization. For example, the complex $BF_3 \cdot H_2O$ catalyzes the polymerization of isobutylene to form polyisobutylene. In the equations that follow, M represents additional monomer groups.

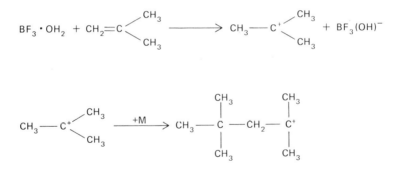

and so on . . .

If R+ is the cation, this reaction may be generalized as follows:

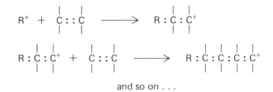

and so on . . .

In anionic polymerization, the double bond in the monomer molecule is attacked by an anion—an atom or group bearing an unshared pair of electrons. Anions are negatively charged because there are more electrons than protons contained in the particle. Alkali metals, amides such as potassium amide (KNH_2), and other compounds are common anionic substances. In the case of potassium amide as the catalyst, the anion is formed and the polymerization initiated as follows. Once again, we will let X represent the monomer molecule.

$$KNH_2 \longrightarrow K^+ + NH_2^-$$
$$NH_2^- + X \longrightarrow NH_2X^-$$
$$NH_2X^- + X \longrightarrow NH_2XX^-$$

and so on . . .

The attack on the double bond in anionic polymerization may be generalized as follows, with R^- representing the anion:

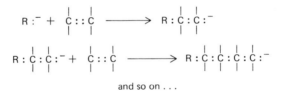

and so on . . .

Types of Polymers

So far we have been discussing polymers made up of organic monomers. Does it surprise you to find that there are other types? Today, three general types are recognized: *inorganic, organometallic,* and *organic.*

Organic polymers are undoubtedly the best understood. They are characterized by the long chains of carbon atoms that make up the backbones of the polymer molecules. These are today's familiar plastics. They include polyethylene, polypropylene, many synthetic fabrics, and synthetic rubbers.

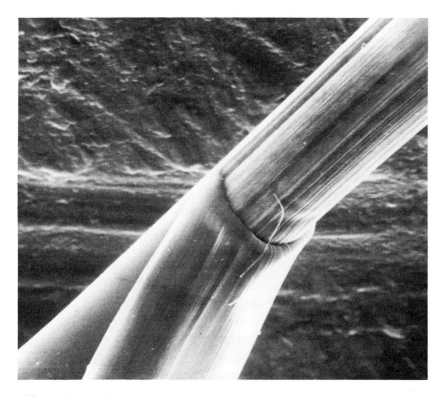

Figure 10-3.   The internal structure of man-made polymer fibers is best studied by "peeling." The fiber is nicked with a razor blade, and the upper part peeled back. Polyester (above) peels in layers like an onion. (Photo courtesy of E. I. du Pont de Nemours and Company, Inc.)

Inorganic polymers do not contain carbon-carbon bonds in their long-chain molecules. The silicates, networks and sheets of silicon and oxygen atoms, the polyphosphates, and boron nitride are examples of inorganic polymers.

Organometallic polymers are a cross between the organic and inorganic types. They do not have carbon-carbon bonds in the molecular backbone, but they do have them in the side chains. There are many different types of organometallic polymers. Those sketched in Figure 10-4 are but a few of the types being studied today.

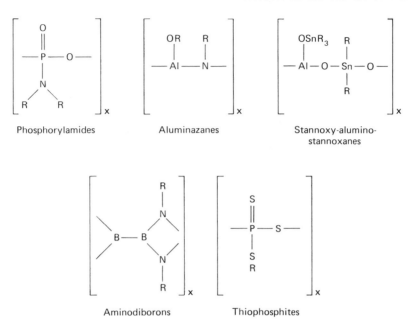

Figure 10-4. Some different types of organometallic polymers. These substances lack carbon-carbon bonds in the molecular backbone, although they are present in the side chains.

Why are they being studied? Think of the many desirable properties of organic polymers—they may be elastic, plastic, very tough, or resistant to corrosion, for example. But they are not generally stable to excessive heat. Inorganic polymers, on the other hand, are heat resistant. They are also brittle, hard, and often quite unworkable. The aim of this research, then, is to combine the desirable properties of the two types of compounds.

The only worthwhile organometallic polymers available today are the *silicones*. A wide variety of applications for these compounds has been developed. Intensive study of the organic chemistry of silicon dates back to the turn of the century. About that time scientists synthesized compounds called di-alkyl-dichlorosilanes, and investigated *hydrolysis*, their chemical behavior with water.

It was thought that compounds of this type would hydrolyze to substances quite analogous to ketones. Hence the term *silicone* was applied to the hydrolysis products. It was noted shortly, however, that the chlorosilanes do not hydrolyze to ketonelike compounds. The chemistry of silicon will help us better understand these substances.

Silicon, in the same family of elements as carbon, could be expected to have chemical properties very similar to those of carbon. The silicon atom, however, is much larger, and there is a greater screening of the nuclear charge. Silicon does, however, form tetrahedral bonds. The structure of silicon dioxide is a good example. As you saw in Chapter Three, this structure can be described as each silicon atom being surrounded by four oxygen atoms, and each oxygen atom being bonded to two silicon atoms.

This network can be described as a series of spiraling silicon-oxygen chains cross-linked with each other by oxygen bonds.

Now, when chlorosilanes are hydrolyzed, the products polymerize to give compounds with the same type of molecular backbone, the —Si—O—Si— structure. In the following example, R is an organic radical. The most common radicals are methyl and phenyl groups. The starting material is a di-alkyl-dichlorosilane, and the final polymer is the straight-chain type.

Because the molecular backbone is the same as in the silicon dioxide structure, there are certain common properties. Indeed, the synthesis of this type of compound opened up the field of organometallic polymers. Chemists realized that in these compounds it is possible to combine the useful properties of both organic and inorganic substances.

The substituted chlorosilanes, general formula $R_xSiCl_{(4-x)}$, are the starting materials for the preparation of silicones. The simplest chlorosilane is tetrachlorosilane, $SiCl_4$. When this compound is hydrolyzed, the silicon dioxide structure is the result.

Chemists have found that it is possible to "tailor" the preparation of silicones with special properties. Let's look at some of the results of this "tailoring."

Silicone oils are composed of straight-chain polymers of varying length. They are quite stable to heat, and change very little in viscosity over a wide temperature range. They are now widely used as lubricants, in hydraulic systems, as high temperature baths, and as heat-transfer media. They are also used to break emulsions, and to suppress foams.

Silicone greases, two-phase systems containing a silicone oil and a thickening agent, are also chemically inert and heat stable. They have found use in a variety of lubrication applications that require a high degree of stability. In addition, they are highly resistant to chemical corrosion.

Heat-hardened *silicone resins* have also been developed, and find useful applications as surface coatings. They have been used as a constituent of paints, varnishes, and auto polishes. Probably the most important use of silicone resins, however, is as insulating materials. Their high heat resistance and chemical stability in particular lend themselves to this use.

Silicone rubbers are unique for their high heat stability, resistance to oxidation, and retention of elasticity down to very low temperatures. These rubbers have been used in shock absorbers, and in gaskets that must withstand very high temperatures.

The silicones are but one example of the interesting new materials coming out of organometallic polymer research. The future holds great promise.

11

MOLECULAR ENGINEERING – Man-Made Molecules to Order

You're an automobile manufacturer, and you're giving orders to the research department. You've told them you want a new polymer to line the walls of the cylinders in gasoline engines. This polymer, to do the job, must be extremely heat and corrosion resistant; it must also lubricate the piston, eliminating the need for oil; it must also resist mechanical wear for at least 100,000 miles of driving. A tall order? Ten years ago you would have been hooted out of the lab; today the research department would probably tell you, "It's possible, but you'll have to wait a bit."

As unrealistic as this demand sounds, it is not so far-fetched, at that. Polymer scientists are on the verge of doing just what is called for in this hypothetical case. Today we know how to do the job, in principle, at least. Tomorrow it will be done in fact.

Clearly, a very thorough knowledge of the structure and properties of polymers must go before the actual design and synthesis of made-to-order substances. Polymer scientists are still studying structure. Next comes the very important job of correlating properties with known structures at the molecular-group level. This is the key to the whole process. When a good one-to-one correlation between these structural factors and properties has been established, the rest will be routine.

The "Materials Revolution"—Here to Stay

No serious observer of the "materials revolution" can doubt the reality of the challenge of plastics to traditional materials. Today plastics substitute for metals, leather, glass, manila and sisal, and drying oils, among others. Tomorrow the pressures of new technologies such as space travel, underwater living, new methods of raising crops, and the problems of feeding an expanding world population will demand new and inexpensive raw materials. Dwindling natural resources plus increasing personal consumption on the part of an increasing world population place even greater demands on polymer scientists. Indeed, people's basic needs alone, such as food, shelter, health, communication, education, transportation, clothing, and recreation will probably provide sufficient impetus to keep the materials revolution moving.

Figure 11-1.   Successful plastic substitute for metal and glass. The front hood and windshield of this snowmobile, as well as other parts, are made of Lexan polycarbonate. This polymer has an impact strength greater than double that of other engineering plastics. (Photo courtesy of GE Plastics Department)

As mentioned, detailed knowledge of the correlation between molecular structure and properties is essential to the engineering of new polymers. Acquiring such knowledge, however, is no mean task. For example, let's look at some of the structural factors in polyethylene ($-CH_2-CH_2-$) that relate to properties. To begin with, it seems clear that the positions of the atoms within the crystalline solid must be known. This can be done by x-ray diffraction, a process that plots the positions of atoms in crystals by passing x-rays through the solid crystal. But the atomic locations found by x-ray diffraction are the equilibrium positions. These are the average positions of the atoms as they vibrate about in three-dimensional space. Figure 11-2 shows the equilibrium positions of the atoms in polyethylene. The dotted line outlines a single unit cell of crystalline polyethylene. A unit cell, you may recall, is the smallest repeating three-dimensional molecular unit within the substance.

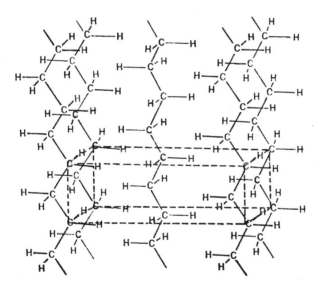

Figure 11-2. The average, or equilibrium positions of the atoms in polyethylene. The dotted line outlines the unit cell of crystalline polyethylene.

Stretching, Twisting, Vibrating

The positions of the atoms alone, however, do not completely describe the solid state. The motions of the atoms must also be considered.

As Figure 11-3 shows, any number of possible motions among the atoms of the CH_2 group are possible. First, as shown in (a) and (b), motions associated with the stretching and contracting of bonds may take place. In (c), a change in bond angle plus a change in bond length is shown. In (d), a twisting of the hydrogen atoms to one side is shown. This movement may also occur in the opposite direction. Finally, in (e) and (f), the electrostatic forces that produce movement are shown. In one, attractive forces pull the hydrogen atoms together, and in the other, repulsive forces drive them apart. Finally, if these CH_2 groups were mounted in a chain, as in polyethylene, the various possible movements would couple with the movements of all other CH_2 groups. The result is a far more complicated system than simple rigid chains lying side by side.

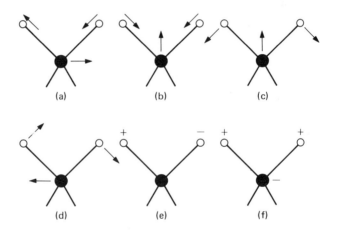

Figure 11-3.   The various possible motions among the atoms of the CH_2 group in polyethylene. Stretching, contracting, bond angle variation, and twisting all occur.

But this does not complete the possible motions of atoms within the solid polyethylene. Three new modes of vibrations are introduced when the CH_2's are linked to each other. Now there are long carbon-to-carbon chains. These chains, most simply represented as —C—C—C —, bend, stretch, and twist. If you picture in your mind all of these possible motions, you will understand the magnitude of the problem. It is indeed "no mean task" to correlate molecular structure with measurable properties in such detail that "tailor-made" molecules may be designed.

Properties and Applications

Several properties are important in polymer applications. For a given application, of course, it is necessary to tailor a specific combination of properties. But this is where the trouble begins, because often the upgrading of one property is correlated with a downgrading of another. For example, when the stiffness of a *thermoplastic* is improved, there is often a loss of toughness. Thermoplastics are substances that can be softened by heat; then, while soft, they can be molded, cast, or extruded under pressure. On cooling, thermoplastics become rigid and retain the shape they were worked into. Heating and cooling of thermoplastics may be repeated over and over again. *Thermosets* are also molded and cast, but unlike thermoplastics, they cannot be reheated after the first application of heat and pressure. An irreversible chemical change takes place during this first application of heat and pressure, and the plastic becomes hard, insoluble, and resistant to melting.

A number of different physical properties have been identified as desirable in plastics. Let's consider the more important of these, and describe some gains that have been made.

Heat Resistance. The object here is to produce stable polymers with very high softening or melting temperatures. Some significant gains have been made, although much remains to be done. PPO (polyphenylene oxide) is an example of a heat resistant polymer. Typical PPO materials are stable between –170°C and 190°C. They can be injection molded, blow molded, and thermoformed, and products can be worked and heated in a variety of ways. Another type of heat resistant plastic is the thermosetting organic polymer, such as the polyimides. These substances retain their mechanical and electrical properties between temperature limits of −190°C and 390°C. Polyimides are difficult to process because of their high viscosity and great thermal stability. They are available only in fabricated form, often in conjunction with glass or carbon fibrous reinforcement. Nonlubricated bearings, seals, and wire coatings are typical applications. In a more exotic application, metallized polyimide film formed the two inner layers of Neil Armstrong's space suit; these layers protected him from lunar temperature extremes when he was out on the moon's surface.

Three general avenues of research are being followed in the effort to produce polymeric substances with higher heat resistance. In one, the point of attack is the active carbon-hydrogen groups found in so many polymers. If these groups can be replaced with others more stable to heat, the overall heat stability should also improve.

Another possibility is replacing carbon in the chain with other types of atoms. The third approach is the synthesis of chains from structures with greater stability than simple carbon chains. These possibilities are illustrated in Figure 11-4. To begin with, double chain polymers show higher resistance to heat. For example, black orlon (a) consists of a double-chain molecule produced from polyacrylonitrile fiber. The ladderlike silicone molecule (b), in which $R=C_6H_5$, is also resistant to heat.

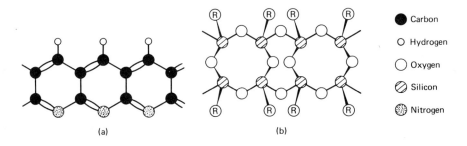

Figure 11-4.   Double-chain (a) and ladderlike (b) polymer molecules show higher resistance to heat.

Rigidity.   Despite great effort in recent years, substances with a high degree of rigidity still elude polymer chemists. As a result, a new approach is being explored. This is the use of reinforcing fibers and filaments. Today reinforced plastics containing glass fibers or asbestos are well known to the engineer and technologist. At present reinforced thermosets are more commonly in use. It is expected that future developments will concentrate on reinforced thermoplastics, largely because of the ease and speed with which thermoplastics can be molded and extruded. Reinforcing with glass or asbestos fibers can increase the stiffness of a thermoplastic by a factor of eight, strength by a factor of three, and heat distortion point by as much as 100°C. Encouraging results such as these have led to a few practical applications, and today you will find reinforced thermoplastics used in such items as gear wheels, appliance cases, instrument bearings, electrical parts, trays, and so on.

Tensile strength.   Is a plastic substance brittle or tough? That is, does it withstand deforming forces and spring back when the force is released, or does it crack and become useless? All of us are familiar with the easily broken plastic object. Indeed, if there has been one basic complaint about plastic objects, it has been the ease with which they are broken. This is a function of tensile strength. Unfortunately, this problem has not really been solved, and with the exception of small objects and the use of reinforced plastics, no generally acceptable strong plastic is available.

Other desirable properties that lack of space prevents us from treating here are *resistance to solvents and swelling agents, elongation to break,* and *resistance to breakdown* from radiation, active chemical reagents, and heat.

Today three major types of polymers are available to the molecular engineer. These substances have proved to be very useful for a large number of applications, but more important, they provide the basis for an interesting approach to newer and even more useful substances.

The first of these substances contains crystallizable polymers with

Figure 11-5.   Clear as glass, dishwasher proof, heat resistant, and stain resistant, this Lexan polycarbonate blender jar is the only unbreakable one available. (Photo courtesy of GE Plastics Department)

flexible chains of molecules. These are good fiber and film formers. They are relatively soluble, may be transparent or opaque, and are thermoplastic.

The second group contains highly cross-linked polymers, substances that are hard, and sometimes brittle. These polymers are thermosetting, usually insoluble and nonswelling, and heat resistant.

The third group contains amorphous thermoplastic resins, a group of macromolecules with inflexible spines. These substances are relatively rigid, and soften at higher temperatures.

Like many new ideas in science, the novel approach to improved polymers described here is utterly simple in principle. To grasp how it works, refer to the diagram in Figure 11-6. Note that one of each of the three groups of polymers has been placed at the vertex of a triangle.

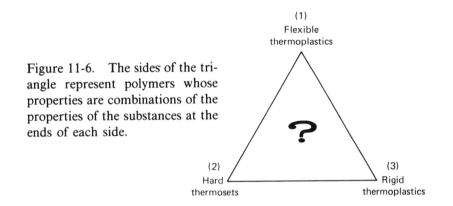

Figure 11-6. The sides of the triangle represent polymers whose properties are combinations of the properties of the substances at the ends of each side.

The sides of the triangle now represent polymers with combinations of the properties of the substances at the ends of each side. For example, consider the side between the first two groups. Structurally, these polymers would contain molecules that are crystallizable and flexible. But they would also be cross-linked to a certain degree. Are there such substances? Yes indeed! Natural rubber and several types of synthetic rubber fall into this group.

Along the line between the first and the third groups, we should expect substances with properties between complete flexibility and stiffness. One such material is cellulose. Cellulose, as you may know, was first synthesized in the laboratory just a few years ago. A number of applications of cellulosic filaments depend upon its intermediacy between complete flexibility and total rigidity.

What properties do you predict for polymers along the line between the second and third groups? And how about the center of the triangle? Here is where the real challenge of the future lies. Today many polymer chemists are devoting all of their time to the synthesis of compounds in this "no man's land." In time we can expect many new polymers with combinations of properties far superior to those available today.

The Problem of Deterioration

So far we have been talking about the positive aspects of molecular engineering—how to build a polymer with specific desirable properties. Unfortunately, this is only half of the story. All polymer substances, despite their many good characteristics, suffer from attack by chemical agents in the environment. Thus, an important task of the polymer chemist is finding a way to build into the molecules themselves protection against weathering and deterioration. Chemical attack and breakdown occur during two phases of a plastic's life—during fabrication into a useful article and during its subsequent use.

During fabrication, plastics are usually heated and then molded or extruded. This heating in air to temperatures as high as several hundred degrees centigrade may lead to chemical changes. During use, however, at predominately ordinary temperatures, changes brought about by heat are less important. The polymer will surely be exposed to sunlight and the atmosphere, however, during use. Thus, photo-oxidative changes may occur. Other agents that attack polymers are moisture, ozone, industrial pollutants, x-rays, gamma rays, and mechanical stresses.

The type of deterioration we are talking about here can take several forms. The polymer may discolor, or the surface may craze, crack, or flake. On the other hand, the structural integrity of the polymer's molecules may be changed chemically, and several important physical properties may be affected as a result. The polymer may, for example, lose its tensile strength, its rigidity, its elasticity, or its electrical insulating properties. Sometimes gaseous decomposition products are formed. When this occurs, it usually indicates a very fundamental change within the polymer's molecular structure. Many of these chemical changes are well understood.

Discoloration can be a very annoying change, especially in objects that have decorative value. One chemical cause is the development of conjugated structures, that is, the appearance of alternating double and single bonds within the polymer molecules.

A common plastic that suffers from discoloration is PVC (polyvinyl chloride). In this case weathering produces the chemical change shown in Figure 11-7.

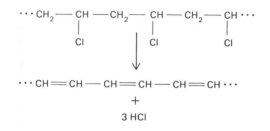

Figure 11-7.   Weathering of polyvinyl chloride (PVC) produces alternating double and single bonds and liberates hydrogen chloride (HCl). The result is discoloration.

Note that HCl, a volatile decomposition product, is released during this reaction, and that alternating double and single bonds are formed. This picture of the discoloration of PVC is far too simple, however. For one thing, the molecular structure of the polymer shown above is highly idealized. There is no information about the nature of the ends of the molecular chains, nor of abnormalities within the molecules themselves. A few such abnormalities are branches in the molecular chains, the presence of double bonds, and partially oxidized structures. All of these, plus others, become built into the substance during formation of the polymer, during fabrication or other processing, and even during storage. All of these abnormalities, even though they are in very low concentrations, constitute "weak points" in the molecules. These molecular flaws are particularly susceptible to what are called "zip" reactions. Once started, zip reactions move from unit to unit along a polymer's molecular chain, often quite rapidly. For example, a single double bond in a PVC molecular chain can lead to rapid decomposition (see Figure 11-8).

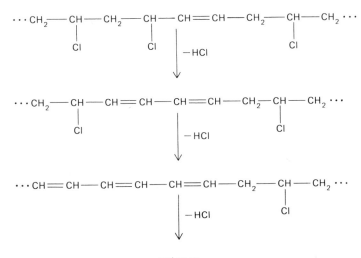

Figure 11-8.   A single double bond in the PVC molecular chain can lead to a "zip" decomposition reaction. Note how the newly formed double bonds move to the left.

Note how the elimination of HCl produces a double bond in the chain; in this case, the zip reaction is moving toward the left.

Sometimes, when a polymer is fabricated at high temperatures, a break may occur in the molecular chain. When this occurs, the polymer can liberate monomer in a reaction just the opposite of formation. In a manner of speaking, the polymer is "unzipping." In the case of polymethylmethacrylate, this reaction goes as shown in Figure 11-9. In each instance, an electron-pair is broken. Electron rearrangement then takes place in each molecular fragment, and monomer molecules are regenerated.

Of course, prior to rearrangement of the electrons each fragment is a free radical—a particle carrying an unpaired electron. Free radicals are important in many different types of deterioration reactions. The energy of sunlight, for example, is sufficient to break bonds in polyethy-

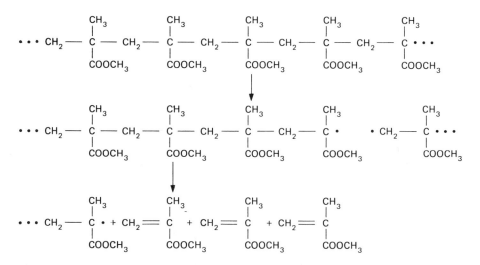

Figure 11-9. The break (second line) in the molecular chain of polymethylmethacrylate can trigger the liberation of monomer molecules in a sort of unzipping reaction.

lene, producing free radicals as a result. See Figure 11-10. Oxygen of the air then reacts strongly with the free radicals.

Figure 11-10. The energy of sunlight can break bonds in polyethylene, producing free radicals. These then react with oxygen of the air, leading to deterioration of the polymer.

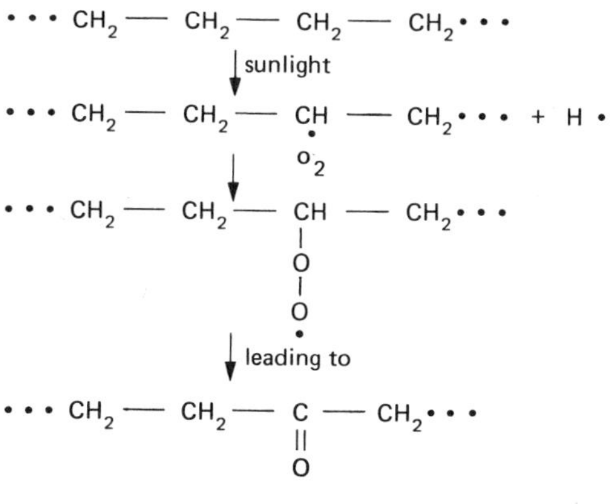

But the carbonyl groups (C=O) absorb sunlight very strongly, and the deterioration reactions are accelerated. Pure polyethylene is an exceptionally fine electrical insulator. Indeed, many of its more important uses are based on this property. Deteriorated polyethylene containing numerous carbonyl groups, however, is a poor insulator. The problem is that this sort of deterioration is not obvious to the naked eye. Thus, a polyethylene insulator can become a hazard in high voltage applications.

Purely structural changes that weaken a plastic may also occur. For example, if a polymer chain is broken into fragments during weathering, the mechanical properties of the plastic will be affected.

$$\ldots X-X-X-X-X-X-X-X \ldots \longrightarrow X-X-X+X-X-X+X-X$$

Other possibilities include the formation of new chemical linkages between molecular chains:

$$
\begin{array}{c}
X-X-\underset{|}{X}-X-X-X-X-X \\
X-X-X-X-X-\underset{|}{X}-X-X \\
X-X-X-X-X-X-X-X
\end{array}
$$

Under these circumstances, the molecules.are held rigidly in position relative to each other. Controlled cross-linking is often desirable, as in the vulcanization of rubber. Uncontrolled cross-linking, however, leads to embrittlement.

How does the molecular engineer cope with these difficulties? He begins by acquiring a thorough understanding of all of the possible deterioration reactions. When this information is combined with detailed knowledge of the fine molecular structure of the polymer under study, corrective steps may be taken. Among these steps are the following. First, the process by which the polymer is manufactured can be refined so that the product contains a minimum of structural abnormalities—the chain branches, double bonds, free radicals, and partially oxidized groups that are so susceptible to chemical attack and deterioration.

A second possibility is the insertion of "blocking" groups into the molecular structure of the polymer. These groups would serve to block "zip" reactions; since they consist of a different molecular group from the backbone monomer they would not enter into the zip reaction. For example, the addition of a small amount of ethyl acrylate (A) to the polymer methyl methacrylate (M) during its production distributes the

Figure 11-11.   An example of the impact of polymers on mid-twentieth century life. These graduates demonstrate the action of polymer flocculants in the removal of suspended solids from waste water. The first graduate shows untreated waste water. In the second, imposition of an electrical current causes the suspended solids to form flocs. These then float to the surface (right) and are skimmed off. (Photo courtesy of Swift and Company)

ethyl acrylate units at random throughout the polymer:

$$\ldots M-M-M-A-M-M-A-M-M-M \ldots$$

Any zip reaction that starts would then be halted as soon as it reached an ethyl acrylate group.

Finally, and this is the most common method of stabilizing polymers —special chemical additives may be mixed in with the polymer. These substances are selected in terms of the type of deterioration reaction to which the polymer is most susceptible. Thus, they may react with and inactivate free radicals, react with double bonds and convert them to less active groups, and so forth. If the polymer is especially susceptible to light, an additive that strongly absorbs the particularly active wavelength of light may be used.

Putting it all together, polymer chemists are on the threshhold of a new era—we may yet call the sixties and seventies "the polymer age." Today the pursuit of the detailed chemistry of polymers continues— with significant successes in hand. These successes spur and intensify research. Tomorrow the polymer chemist may indeed engineer a polymer to line the cylinder walls of gasoline engines, to serve as the works of a clock, or perhaps even to build a bridge.

12

PETROLEUM–Nature's Storehouse of Chemicals

Any reasonably well informed person would agree that petroleum is one of the world's most important substances. Starting with crude oil —the form in which petroleum is taken from the ground—petroleum's importance extends into virtually every arena of human activity. Well over 3000 products are made from petroleum. It is mentioned in the Bible, and there are records to indicate that asphalt—a petroleum fraction—was used as early as 3800 B.C. Thus, man's interest in this economically vital substance extends far back into history.

Today, however, despite its continued economic importance, storm clouds hover over its use for a variety of reasons. For example, the gasoline engine is under attack as a major polluter of the atmosphere. Will gasoline engines be cleaned up, or will another source of energy provide power for transportation? In another instance, conservationists and others concerned for the environment are outraged over the disastrous effects of oil spills at sea, both from ruptured tankers and from leaks at offshore drilling sites. As an extension of this concern, the Federal Government (as this is being written) has withheld from several major oil companies permission to lay pipe from the newly discovered northern Alaskan oil fields to southern Alaska. Conservationists fear irreversible damage to the environment if the pipes go in. The oil companies, which have paid to the state of Alaska some $900 million for prospecting rights, are deeply concerned about their investment. Perhaps, as you read this chapter, a satisfactory settlement of this impasse will have been achieved. You owe it to your future and to the future of your children to find out if this settlement ignores or protects the environment.

Figure 12-1. The search for petroleum goes on. The survey truck (left) thumps its way across the Libyan desert sending seismic signals into the earth. How these signals are reflected indicates the possibility of oil deposits. At sea, powerful ultrasonic generators (right) send impulses through the water to the sea bed. Fish are not harmed by these impulses. (Photos courtesy of Raytheon Company)

Petroleum is not only the source of many important industrial chemicals; it also serves as the starting point for an increasing number of derived chemicals. In general, petroleum consists largely of hydrocarbons, with molecules containing from 1 to 50 or more carbon atoms. These molecules exist in a wide variety of types, as we shall see later. Petroleum also contains small amounts of sulfur, nitrogen, oxygen, and metal-containing compounds. Petroleum hydrocarbons, however, are the important raw materials for science and industry. Let's explore the current view of the origin of petroleum. Then we will look into some interesting facts about its composition, and finish by considering the rapidly expanding petrochemicals field.

Origin and Composition

Most authorities agree that the ultimate source material of petroleum was organic, and that sedimentary processes were involved in its formation. There has been some speculation about an inorganic origin of petroleum, but this point of view is now generally disregarded. Evidence also points to the conclusion that marine sediments make up the bulk of petroleum-forming substances.

The original organic matter from which petroleum derived could have included all marine plants and animals. Although there is still some debate on the nature of this substance, many scientists now regard plankton as representative of the raw material from which petroleum was formed. Plankton is the most abundant organic substance in the sea; it serves also as the basic food for higher organisms. It seems reasonable, therefore, to regard it as representative.

Plankton organisms contain essentially the same chemical compounds as higher forms: carbohydrates, proteins, fats, and assorted minerals. Interestingly, traces of hydrocarbons have been found in diatoms, a microscopic plant form. When plankton organisms die, they are either eaten or they sink to the bottom, becoming part of the marine sediment. This slimy sediment, consisting largely of organic debris derived from marine plants and animals, is called *sapropel.* Sapropel is now regarded as the parent substance of petroleum, corresponding to peat as the parent substance of coal.

The chemical environment in existence during petroleum formation could not have been oxidative. Reducing conditions must have prevailed, for oxidation would have converted the organic matter of the sediments into carbon dioxide and water quite rapidly. The environment also must have been uninhabitable for those animals that feed on dead organic matter.

These conditions are met in the many stagnant basins and troughs on the ocean floor. Here anaerobic bacteria decompose the marine sediments, producing the putrified slime, sapropel. The conversion of sapropel to petroleum is thought to involve both inorganic and bio-chemical processes, although the relative part of each is not thoroughly understood.

Bacterial action appears to play a part in the conversion of carbohy-drates and proteins into chemical intermediates, which may then change into hydrocarbons. The following simplified equation describes this process.

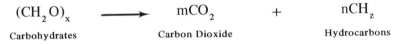

$$(CH_2O)_x \longrightarrow mCO_2 + nCH_z$$

Carbohydrates   Carbon Dioxide   Hydrocarbons

This reaction is a reciprocal oxidation and reduction. Part of the car-bohydrate is oxidized to CO_2 and part reduced to hydrocarbons. Keep in mind, however, that this schematic equation is much oversimplified. The real reactions are certainly more complex, and are still not com-pletely understood.

A possible reaction involving fats has also been worked out. In this example the researchers started with cholesterol, a complex animal fat.

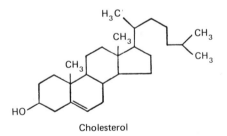

Cholesterol

Cholesterol samples were heated in the presence of sulfur to a tempera-ture of 150°C. The reactions that took place during this treatment yielded aromatic hydrocarbons related to benzene, naphthalene, and phenanthrene, all constituents of petroleum crude.

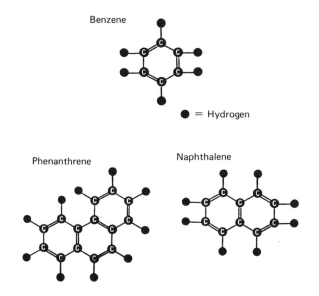

Figure 12-2. The structural formulas of benzene, phenanthrene, and naphthalene. Substances similar to these are produced when cholesterol is heated in the presence of sulfur.

This result is taken as evidence that petroleum hydrocarbons probably originated in part from animal fats. Similar evidence supports the idea that plant matter is also a precursor of petroleum.

The recent finding of hydrocarbons in relatively new marine sediments has caused a complete re-evaluation of the time factor in petroleum formation. It was formerly believed that the formation of crude is an extremely slow process, dating back at least to the Pliocene. The oils recently found, however, have proved (by carbon-14 dating) to be only about 10,000 years old. Thus it appears that petroleum formation requires much less time than previously thought.

The composition of petroleum crudes from different parts of the world has helped unravel the story of its origin. Significantly, all crude oils have about the same elementary composition. This is summarized as follows.

Carbon	83-87%
Hydrogen	11-14%
Oxygen, nitrogen, sulfur and traces of other elements	up to 5%
Ash	0.001-0.05%

As you can see from this breakdown, many crude oils contain 99 percent or more carbon and hydrogen alone. Thus, in terms of elementary composition, petroleum is a simple and fairly uniform substance.

Families of Hydrocarbons

From the standpoint of the number of compounds present in petroleum, however, the picture is quite different. Great variability and complexity are possible. To date, over 175 different hydrocarbon compounds have been isolated from petroleums. Fortunately, however, these compounds all fall into three general classes, or *homologous series.* As you may know, a homologous series is a group of organic compounds each member of which differs from the next by the addition of a —CH_2— group to the molecule. Such series may be represented by general formulas, and usually show gradual but regular changes in properties as molecular weight increases.

The diagrams in Figure 12-3 show skeleton formulas of representative types of compounds found in petroleums. The paraffins may be represented by the general formula C_nH_{2n+2}. The naphthenes, or cycloparaffins, are unsaturated ring compounds with the general formula C_nH_{2n}. Finally, the aromatic, or benzenoid hydrocarbons are represented by the general formula C_nH_{2n-6}. Different crudes contain differing amounts of these three basic types of compounds. Hence, they are distinguished as *paraffinic, naphthenic,* or *benzenoid,* depending upon which type is present in the greatest quantity.

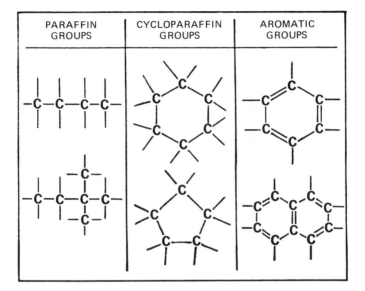

Figure 12-3. Skeleton formulas of the types of compounds found in petroleum crudes.

Even the largest hydrocarbon molecules found in petroleum are too small to be seen with an ordinary microscope. They are very large, however, compared to the size of an atom. For example, the diameter of a hydrogen atom is about 2 angstrom units (2×10^{-8}cm). The carbon atom, which is about 12 times as heavy, nevertheless has roughly the same diameter as a hydrogen atom. Now consider a representative hydrocarbon molecule. Its empirical formula might be $C_{20}H_{42}$. Such a molecule would have a volume of more than 1,000 cubic angstrom units. Its length might be 80 angstrom units (8×10^{-7}cm), or about 40 times the diameter of a hydrogen atom.

Chemical Stability

The stability of the three basic types of hydrocarbons found in petroleum crudes differs. The paraffins are the most stable at lower temperatures. Within any homologous series the fewer the carbon atoms, the greater the stability. Methane (CH_4) is the most stable hydrocarbon in the paraffin series. Cycloparaffin hydrocarbons are roughly as stable as paraffins. The aromatic hydrocarbons are less stable than the corresponding saturated (no double bonds) hydrocarbons. If these chemical facts are taken as criteria, then most petroleum samples are not at a state of maximum stability. In fact, evidence suggests that the older the crude, the more stable it is. Of course, the quantities of saturated, low-molecular-weight compounds present in crude are the major clues to stability. The greater the percentage of paraffins and low-molecular-weight hydrocarbons, the greater the stability.

Since 1930 there has been a spectacular growth in the manufacture of "petrochemicals," the term now used to designate chemicals derived from petroleum fractions. Two factors influenced this growth. First was the relative cheapness of hydrocarbon raw materials. Secondly, expanding plastics, textiles, synthetic rubber, synthetic detergents, and oil additive industries placed heavy demands on the chemical industry for needed chemicals.

Today the majority of petrochemicals are obtained by processing the gaseous fraction of petroleum, as well as from the gaseous products of catalytic cracking. As mentioned, well over 3000 chemical end products are now turned out.

Of all the hydrocarbon raw materials used today, ethylene ($CH_2{=}CH_2$) is by far the most important for chemical production. Over two billion pounds of ethylene are used every year for the production of many important chemicals. These include ethyl alcohol, ethyl benzene, ethyl chloride, and polyethylene plastics.

Ethyl alcohol (C_2H_5OH), for example, was made exclusively for many years from sugars and starches by the fermentation of yeast. Increased demand, however, for its use as a solvent and as a reaction intermediate made it necessary to find a new source that would give a

Figure 12-4. Three-dimensional scale model of a petroleum processing plant. Such models are built prior to actual construction to verify the positioning of piping, valves, pumps, access ladders, and other details. The model pulls together details shown on hundreds of different drawings. (Photo courtesy of Raytheon Company)

high volume yield. This source was ethylene. Today over 90 percent of ethyl alcohol produced in the United States is manufactured from ethylene.

Proteins from Petroleum

In an entirely different area, petroleum crude is now used as the starting raw material for the production of edible proteins and vitamins. Sound strange? Perhaps it is. And yet, when we look at the situation from the point of view of energy, it doesn't seem very strange at all.

Hydrocarbon molecules are energy rich. Thus, we should not be surprised to find that certain microorganisms feed on petroleum crude and convert it to high quality protein. In addition, other microbes will grow on coal tar hydrocarbons, further expanding the potential of this unique source of protein.

Processes of this type are of great interest to nutrition scientists, for they offer a possible solution to the worldwide protein shortage that has plagued mankind for as long as history has been recorded. For example, some of these microbes can turn out edible, high-quality protein 2500 times faster than domestic meat animals. Representative figures go as follows: One cow, weighing 1100 pounds and grazing on pasture, can turn grass into protein (meat) at the rate of only 1.1 pounds per day. But 1100 pounds of microbes, pasturing on hydrocarbons, can produce 2750 pounds of edible protein per day. The protein substance synthesized by microbes might be added to conventional foods as a supplement, or it could be used to help meet human nutritional needs indirectly as a protein supplement for livestock.

Chemically speaking, a protein is a long-chain nitrogenous substance composed mainly of amino acid residues joined by peptide bonds. This is illustrated in Figure 12-5. Here two amino acids (R and R' represent organic side groups) are shown forming a peptide bond by the joint elimination of water from the —NH_2 group of one and the —COOH group of the other. The result is a dipeptide. Many amino acids joined this way make up a polypeptide. The formula at the bottom represents a protein. R* may be one of about 25 different organic side groups. Protein molecular weights are usually in excess of 10,000 and run up into the millions.

From the standpoint of human nutrition, there are two kinds of proteins; complete and incomplete. A complete protein contains all of the eight amino acids essential for growth and maintenance. An incomplete protein is deficient in one or more of these essential amino acids.

In general, complete proteins occur in meat, fish, and animal products. Incomplete proteins occur in plants or seeds. For maximum health and growth, man must have an adequate supply of complete proteins in his diet. Or, alternatively, a carefully selected mixture of incomplete

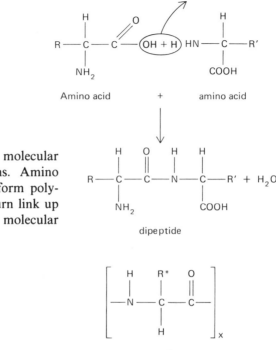

Figure 12-5. The molecular structure of proteins. Amino acids are joined to form poly-peptides. These in turn link up to form the long molecular chains of proteins.

proteins from plant sources will suffice. In either case, the essential amino acids must be supplied.

It is an unfortunate fact that the production of complete protein by raising livestock is quite inefficient. Raising animals for meat depends on plant growth. Plant growth in turn depends on space, soil conditions, the availability of water and fertilizers, and suitable climatic conditions. In addition, plant growth depends on the world's solar energy income.

To date, *man has not been able to find a way to produce food without ultimately relying on solar energy!*

Most modern research efforts have been aimed at better use of this energy income. Thus, we have improvements in animal husbandry, agricultural practices, and food processing.

Now, however, it seems possible to tap the chemical energy trapped in petroleum and coal-tar hydrocarbons when they were formed from ancient plants and animals. Thus, this promising method of protein production utilizes solar energy bound up by living organisms millions of years ago. It is an entirely new concept in food production.

There are many advantages to the use of microorganisms for the synthesis of large complex molecules such as proteins. Microorganisms are very efficient chemical producers. They break down and synthesize complex molecules with ease, and they are not especially demanding as far as environment is concerned. They can live at ordinary temperatures, and their biochemical processes waste very little energy.

The pioneering work that led to protein synthesis began with the identification and isolation of organisms that feed on petroleum components. Then, by gradually altering the chemical nature of the food supply, strains were selected or bred to grow on the least valuable and commercially usable crude-oil fractions. Two essential ingredients, however, were missing. Both *nitrogen* and *oxygen* had to be added so that the microorganisms could synthesize protein.

Now refer to the pilot process diagram shown in Figure 12-6. As you can see, the oxygen is supplied from the air. A source of nitrogen must be added to the batch. This is usually some form of fertilizer, made up in solution. After a suitable period of growth, the batch mixture is centrifuged to separate the solid protein concentrate.

This is followed by a washing step, another centrifugation, and finally controlled drying. The product is isolated in powder form. It may then be fed to meat animals as a feed additive.

This pilot process is a very efficient one. The oxygen is obtained from the air. Nitrogen is supplied in the fertilizer solution. Moreover, the nitrogen is utilized in this process to a much higher degree than in agricultural meat production. *The yield of protein concentrate is almost 100 percent.* That is, for every pound of hydrocarbon supplied to the microorganisms, very nearly a pound of protein concentrate is produced. Add to these efficiency factors the fact that the least desirable hydrocarbon fractions are used in the process, and the significance of this process for a protein-starved world is clear.

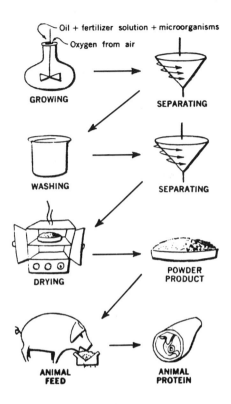

Figure 12-6. Pilot process for preparing protein from petroleum. See the text for details.

What about the nutritional value of the vitamin-protein concentrate? Yes indeed, the concentrate does contain essential vitamins as well as proteins. Studies to date show that the amino acid content is equal to that of plant protein, and as good as most animal proteins. Will proteins from petroleum play a major role in stemming worldwide protein starvation? Only time and further research will tell. One thing, however, is certain. Whether it is proteins from petroleum, fish protein concentrate (FPC), or something else, a cheap nutritious, and easy to use protein source must be made available or the mid-70s will witness worldwide human starvation on a scale never before experienced by man.

13

COAL – A New Source of Chemicals?

The earth's fossil fuels are running out! This is the oft heard cry of industrial pessimists who foresee the day when there will be no more natural gas, petroleum, or coal to drive the wheels of industry. Clearly, our fossil fuels will run out some day. In the meantime, however, estimates give us several hundred years to find alternate sources of power. But this isn't the entire story. It should also be noted that some scientists believe that coal and petroleum are still being formed by sedimentary processes.

Coal is of special interest to chemists today, for its use as a fuel is in decline. As other forms of fuel, such as oil and natural gas, replace coal, chemists have started to probe its structural secrets in the hopes that exciting new uses and chemicals will be discovered. To appreciate this situation—that is, why there is such a strong interest in a dirty, messy, outdated fuel—you'll need to know something about the geochemistry of coal.

The term "fossil fuel" refers to the fact that coal and petroleum, as well as other combustible deposits, are the result of extensive biological activity and sedimentation during the Carboniferous Age. These deposits are often called *bioliths.*

There are two classes of biolithic deposits—the noncombustible (acaustobioliths) and the combustible (caustobioliths). Limestone is the most important noncombustible deposit to come from biological activity. Others, including chert, iron salts, and sulfur have also been identified.

The Origin of Coal

At the time of the Carboniferous Age, conditions were favorable for plant growth. Thick forests, massive growths of ferns of many different types, and great swamps persisted over long periods of time. Coal was formed by the compacting and chemical alteration of plants such as these. To understand fully the origin of coal, however, three basic questions must be answered: (1) What was the nature and composition of the original plants? (2) How did the organic debris from these plants accumulate? (3) What chemical reactions transformed this organic debris into the substance we recognize as coal today?

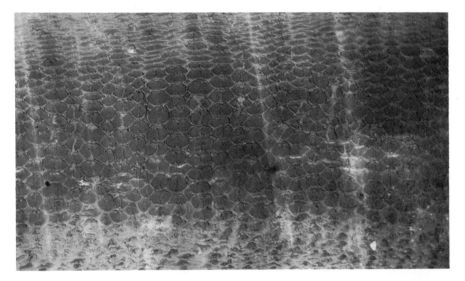

Figure 13-1.   A thin section of vitrain, showing the cell structure of a coalified woody stem. Vitrain is the result of wood preserved initially under water. (Photo courtesy of the Illinois State Geological Survey)

As indicated above, coal is formed by the compacting and partial decomposition of terrestrial plant remains. This plant debris accumulated and was preserved by being covered over later by additional beds of geologic materials. Shales, limestones, and sandstones, for example, are often found above layers of coal. Most coal beds are found in the same location in which the plants grew. The evidence for this is the flat, unrolled condition of fossilized leaves, old stumps with roots still present in the soil below, and the absence of other sediments in the coal layer.

The plant material from which coal derived consisted primarily of *cellulose* and *lignin,* plus a great variety of other minor components. The empirical formulas for cellulose and lignin are $C_6H_{10}O_5$ and $C_{12}H_{18}O_9$. Note that the two substances have about the same percent composition.

Lignin, unlike cellulose, is made up of ringlike groups of carbon atoms. Because of these rings, it is said to be aromatic. Cellulose, however, consists of long chains of $C_6H_{10}O_5$ groups. Coals consist largely of carbon-ring systems, with the six-membered ring most common. Thus, lignin probably contributed directly to coal formation, but cellulose had to be converted chemically to aromatic (ring) compounds.

But this makes the story seem much too simple. It is really far more complex, and not thoroughly understood. For example, the nitrogen content of coal is much higher than that of plants. How do chemists account for this difference? It has been suggested that bacterial action plays a major role in the first stages of coal formation. Thus bacteria, with about 13 percent nitrogen content, could account for the extra nitrogen.

It is thought that the transition from vegetation to coal involves two steps; one biochemical, the other metamorphic. During the biochemical stage, the organic matter is altered by the action of microorganisms. But this phase of the process stops when conditions become unsuitable for bacterial activity. This may be caused by burial under additional sediments or by the development of toxic substances within the organic matter itself.

The result of this bacterial activity is a complex mixture of organic substances—*humus.* It seems likely that coals with different compositions result from the biochemical stage, or, put another way, from the chemical activities of different species of bacteria.

Starting with wood, the progressive stages resulting in anthracite coal are as follows: *wood—peat—lignite—bituminous coal—anthra-*

cite coal. These stages are easily detected by chemical analysis. Chemically, this transition is mainly an increase in carbon along with a decrease in oxygen. Hydrogen also decreases, but less rapidly than oxygen.

Following the biochemical stage, metamorphism occurs. Quite obviously, radical physical and chemical changes take place during this part of the process. Intense heat and pressure seem to be the major driving forces in the metamorphism of coal. Unfortunately, however, even though we are very familiar with the composition of the successive materials in coal formation, very little is known about the actual chemical changes that take place.

The concept of *rank,* that is, the stages lignite, bituminous, or anthracite, designates the degree of metamorphism a coal has undergone. Thus it is an indication of a given coal's stage of development. Some of the geological factors that may determine the rank of a coal are the following: (1) The length of time of burial—many apparent exceptions here have placed this factor in doubt. (2) The action of heat. (3) The action of increased pressure.

Importance of Composition of Coal

Much is known about the chemical composition of coal. This information, of course, is vitally important, for it is the key to new uses for coal and new chemicals from coal. At this point, we will briefly review coal's chemical composition. Following this review, let's look into a hypothetical model for the structural chemistry of bituminous coal, and relate this structure to the search for new coal-derived chemicals.

Coal consists primarily of complex organic compounds of high molecular weight. These compounds are mostly aromatic. Moreover, the higher the rank of the coal, the greater the number of ring compounds. The evidence indicates that six-membered carbon rings are the most common. The highest rank possible corresponds to graphite, which is completely aromatic. The oxygen content of coal is present in the form of —COOH and —OH groups. During rank increase, oxygen is given off in the form of water and carbon dioxide. The hydrogen content of coal drops sharply between bituminous and anthracite. This occurs because large amounts of methane (CH_4) are expelled during this stage of metamorphism. Nitrogen is found in coal either as amino groups (—NH_2) or substituted for carbon in the ring structures.

The following table sets out representative compositions for various ranks of coal. Keep in mind that a mixture such as coal does not have a fixed composition. These figures represent an average, and not the precise composition of any given coal.

PERCENT COMPOSITION OF TYPICAL COALS

Rank	C	H	N	O
Lignite	72.4	5.3	1.1	20.5
Subbituminous	77.7	5.2	1.6	15.0
High Volatile Bituminous	81.8	5.3	1.8	10.2
Low Volatile Bituminous	91.4	4.6	1.2	2.1
Anthracite	94.9	1.8	0.7	1.8

Any investigation of coal to discover new chemicals must involve a nondestructive method to take the coal apart. After all, coal is a mixture. Thus, the logical starting point is separation and identification of its numerous chemical components. The process by which this is accomplished is called *carbonization.*

Carbonization involves heating coal in the absence of air: it produces very smelly, but nevertheless interesting mixtures of smoky vapors and liquid tars. These mixtures result from the thermal decomposition of the large molecules in the coal substance. They contain various gases, tars, and water vapor. Today the only chemicals obtained from coal come from these carbonization by-products.

Chemical Potential Not Yet Realized

Chemists, however, agree that full utilization of the chemical potential of coal has not been achieved. The gases, light oils, tars, and ammoniacal liquors derived from the carbonization process are certainly important. What is now needed is a new approach to the whole problem. Intensive study of the molecular structure of coal may open the way. Given a detailed knowledge of structure, the next step should be a matter of time only. Thus, it is conceivable that we may soon see coal the basic raw material for a large number of industrially important chemicals.

Concentrated research on the molecular structure of coal did not begin until some 15 to 20 years ago. Much progress has been made since then, although the structure of coal is still less well understood than the structures of many other natural substances.

Infrared spectroscopy shows that most of the hydrogen in coals is bonded to carbon in aliphatic structures. As you recall, aliphatic hydrocarbons occur in both chains and rings, but the bonding between carbons is the delocalized electron-cloud bond found in the benzene ring. Aliphatic structures in coal have now been clarified.

We know today that they are a very special type. Dehydrogenation (removal of hydrogen) studies indicate that they are mostly *hydroaromatic* rings, ring molecules having many aliphatic properties, but capable of becoming aromatic by the simple loss of hydrogen.

The diagram in Figure 13-2 shows the probable molecular structure of a fragment of a typical bituminous coal. Note the number of rings that are nearly aromatic—these are the hydroaromatic rings; they contain only two double bonds. Note also how the hydroaromatic rings seem to link the aromatic rings (three double bonds) together.

There is strong evidence that the major structural feature of coal is aromatic rings. Apparently, these rings occur in groups, with two to three benzene rings fused together to form an aromatic nucleus. Also, as mentioned, the evidence suggests that the hydroaromatic rings link the aromatic nuclei together in coal.

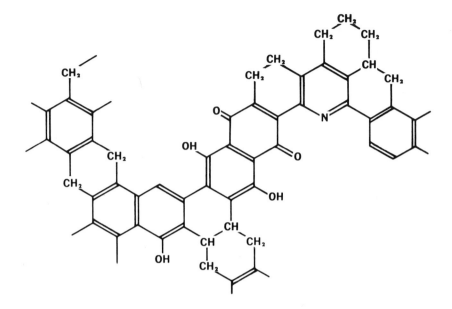

Figure 13-2.   The probable molecular structure of a fragment of a typical bituminous coal.

All coals contain a significant amount of chemically combined oxygen. Today, through infrared spectroscopy combined with functional
group analysis, we understand the chemical nature of most of this
oxygen. A good part of it is tied up in phenolic hydroxyl groups. Phenol
is simply benzene with a hydroxyl group substituted for one of the
hydrogen atoms (C_6H_5OH). Can you locate these phenolic hydroxyl
groups in Figure 13-2?

The oxygen also occurs in carbonyl groups. The carbonyl group is
the divalent organic radical C=O. Locate some of these groups in the
diagram. The total amount of carbon in the cyclic systems in coal is not
known exactly, although available evidence puts it at about 65-85 percent.

Coal and Industry's Needs

Knowing something about the structure of coal, the next question is: What chemicals does industry need most?

The answer to this question lies in the phenomenal growth of synthetics over the past 20 years. World War II provided the initial impetus; the rest is history.

But interestingly enough, the great majority of these new man-made substances are produced from a very small number of chemical raw materials. Today these basic chemicals cannot be obtained economically from coal. Most of them are derived from natural gas or petroleum. Table 13-1 illustrates some of these chemical building blocks, and lists some of the products they go into. This, however, is by no means an exhaustive list.

TABLE 13-1. RAW MATERIALS FOR SYNTHETIC CHEMICALS,
PLUS SOME OF THE PRODUCTS THEY ARE USED IN.

Product	*Basic Chemical Raw Materials*
Alcohol	Ethylene
Aspirin	Toluene
Antifreeze (ethylene glycol)	Ethylene
Latex (emulsion) paints	Benzene, butadiene, ethylene
Nylon	Benzene, some butadiene
Orlon	Acetylene, some ethylene
Polyethylene	Ethylene
Synthetic detergents	Benzene, propylene
Synthetic rubber	Benzene, butadiene, ethylene, acetylene

The synthetic chemical industry wants a guaranteed supply of the basic chemicals it has learned to use so effectively. But this must also be an inexpensive supply.

Coal may be one answer. For example, look again at the diagram of the probable structure of bituminous coal. Benzene, phenol, and naphthalene are much in demand. And they all occur in bound-up form in the structure of coal. Getting them out, however, is another story. The exact bonding by which they are tied up in coal is not as yet understood. Hence the problem, simply put, is how can coal be decomposed to yield these highly desirable breakdown products?

One approach is controlled decomposition. In general, this would include carefully monitored reactions and the removal of decomposition products as they form. Selective oxidation might be tried. Thus, the aliphatic portion of the coal structure would be oxidized away to carboxyl groups, leaving behind the aromatic nuclei. Unfortunately, a number of factors stand in the way of this method.

First, some of the aromatic groups might be attacked, reducing the total aromatic yield. Second, some of the hydroaromatic rings would be oxidized to molecules resistant to further oxidation. Finally, it appears that separation of the oxidation products would be too difficult and expensive.

Hydrogenolysis, or coal hydrogenation, has been carried out on a fairly large scale in Europe to manufacture liquid fuels and various chemical by-products. Unfortunately, as a source of chemical raw materials this process of saturation and fragmentation of ring structures to produce simple aliphatics is far too expensive.

Careful analysis of all possibilities has led chemists to the reluctant conclusion that controlled breakdown is not the answer. All available processes are both too difficult to control adequately and much too expensive. The answer, if there is one, lies in some other approach.

One or two possibilities stand out. New carbonization processes, using catalysts and other additives and very rapid heating could give higher chemical yields than present processes. Total gasification of coal has also been suggested. This approach has been investigated very carefully in England. In the final analysis, this may be the answer. Many coal chemists seem to agree that total decomposition to very simple fragments and resynthesis is the only way out.

Coal remains an intriguing challenge to the chemist. It is a substance unbelievably rich in vitally important chemicals. The trick is to find a way to extract these chemicals and use them without destroying their potential during the extraction process. In a time of declining interest in coal as a fuel, we can feel confident that this will eventually take place.

POSTSCRIPT

For those readers who may have found *Molecules in the Service of Man* apparently incomplete, I have this to say. There was no attempt at any time to be all-inclusive. Clearly, there are many additional types of interesting molecules that could have been included in the book. Instead, such matters as the overall length of the book, the probable attention span of the reader, and quite frankly, my great interest in the topics chosen have collectively conspired to produce the chemical potpourri you have just finished reading. I hasten to add, however, that there is some semblance of order in my choices. You've been introduced to both inorganic and organic molecules; to substances with immediate practical applications and others important primarily to the theoretical chemist; to molecules that first seemed miraculous in their value to man, only to turn out later to be serious threats both to man and the environment; and finally, to some of the fantastic possibilities inherent in the application of knowledge of molecular structure.

Perhaps this chemical "stew," derived from the alphabet "soup" of matter—atoms—will broaden your appetite and tempt you to read further in chemistry. If this should come to pass, I will have achieved my purpose. Nothing would please me more.

A.H.D.

INDEX

The Author

A. H. Drummond, Jr. was born in Manhattan, went to college in Maine, and has lived in New York, California, Connecticut, Illinois, and Massachusetts. He majored in science at Bowdoin College, and holds graduate degrees from Hofstra and Wesleyan universities. Formerly a science teacher, Mr. Drummond has also served as an inspector with the U.S. Food and Drug Administration and done industrial chemical work, educational science writing, and textbook editing. He is currently editor-in-chief of a school science department for a major publishing firm.

Mr. Drummond is the author of seven books, including the widely adopted monographs *Atoms-Crystals-Molecules: Modern Views of Atomic Structure, Chemical Bonding, and Molecular Geometry* and *Chemical Reactions: What They Are and How They Occur.* In addition, he has contributed numerous articles to American and British science education journals. When not busy on a book, he can most often be found pursuing his hobbies of restoring and building clocks, and sailing.

Mr. Drummond and his family reside in Bedford, Massachusetts.